"When I began in ministry as a young leader, I lived by this book as our church grew from a handful of people to 200 and then over the years to over 1,000. Everything Carl George and Warren Bird said was bang-on every step of the way. This book has been a lifesaver for me in ministry. So I could not be more thrilled to see that it's being revised and expanded for a new generation of church leaders. I cannot recommend this book highly enough."

Carey Nieuwhof, founding pastor, Connexus Church, Barrie and Orillia, Ontario; blogger, careynieuwhof.com

"The whole goal of ministry is to give it away to more and more people. In Saddleback's early years I invited our people into a covenant, 'If you'll do the ministry, I'll make sure you're well fed.' That turning point transformed our church and led to a season of incredible growth—and this excellent book shows you how to make a similar transition."

Rick Warren, pastor, Saddleback Church, Lake Forest, California; founder, Pastors.com

"What if God wanted you to handle twice as many people as you are ministering to at present? Five times? Ten times? This highly practical book shows you a contagious vision of the harvest God wants to grant to your church. Then it shows you how to put the primary-care pastoral ministry of the church into the hands of lay shepherds who lead small groups."

Chris Hodges, pastor, Church of the Highlands; author, *Fresh Air*

"I wish I had read this book long ago. For too many years my husband and I did all the counseling and care, spread far too thin. Then a pastor friend helped us see the value of raising up and coaching other caregivers. That's what this book does. It saves you heartache, shows you what to do, and multiplies your impact."

Noemi Chavez, copastor, Seventh Street Church, Long Beach, California

"The movements I lead wouldn't be what they are today without the insights and coaching of Carl George. The contents of this book are directly related to everything we do in the multiplication of small groups, new campuses, and networks of reproducing churches."

Dave Ferguson, lead pastor, Community Christian Church, Naperville, Illinois; founder, Exponential Conference; cofounder, NewThing church planting network; coauthor, *Starting Over: Your Life Beyond Regrets*

"If you want to be more effective at empowering others, read this amazing book. Adequate caring, fueled by Holy Spirit–given giftedness, lies at the foundation of all sustainable church growth."

Sam Chand, leadership consultant; author, *Leadership Pain*

"I am excited the book is being updated; I have shared this with many church leaders. Very few books are as effective at clearing away the cobwebs of confusion and enabling ministry leaders to imagine a better future."

Allen Jackson, founding pastor, World Outreach Church, Murfreesboro, Tennessee; coach/author, Intend Ministries

"*How to Break Growth Barriers* unlocks the strategy for pastors to powerfully multiply pastoral care through small group community. When that happens, both pastor and people win, plus more disciples are made."

Allen White, author, *Exponential Groups: Unleashing Your Church's Potential*; church consultant, allenwhite.org

"It was over twenty years ago that I sat in Carl's seminar, 'How to Break Growth Barriers.' It was a revolutionary experience in my thinking about church. When the book came out, I bought it and still have it today—dog-eared and well-marked. I am happy that a new generation of church leaders have an opportunity to benefit from this updated and revised edition. It's still revolutionary!"

Mike Chapman, senior pastor, City Church, Chattanooga, Tennessee

"*How to Break Growth Barriers* is an excellent resource not only for senior pastors but for people at all levels—and especially women in leadership. It skillfully navigates barriers, both external and internal, that hinder growth."

Sherry Surratt, lead author, *Just Lead! A Practical Guide for Women Leaders in the Church*

"The wise counsel found in these pages will be of inestimable value to everyone who loves and seeks to serve the church."

Ted Engstrom, president emeritus, World Vision

"A momentous book that will become the textbook in how to break growth barriers."

Dale Galloway, pastor, New Hope Community Church, Portland, Oregon

"The disarming thing about Carl George is how he blends the science of church growth (if there is such a thing) with the spirit of church growth (and there is such a thing). That 'spirit' is the Holy Spirit, and I'm grateful for Carl's emphasis as we seek ways to partner with the Savior who is building His church so wondrously today."

Jack Hayford, pastor, Church on the Way, Van Nuys, California; www.jackhayford.org

"I particularly like Carl George's emphasis on the ministry of all people. In this, he stands in the line of Martin Luther and Elton Trueblood."

Kenneth C. Haugk, founder and executive director, Stephen Ministries

"The author has offered compelling reasons why care givers must find a new way of caring. The needs are too great and the world is too complex to go on with business as usual."

Bill Hinson, pastor, First United Methodist Church, Houston, Texas

"The book commands 'must-read' status for all who do ministry and teach others to do ministry."

John W. Reed, chairman, pastoral ministries department, Dallas Theological Seminary

"Carl George is both prophetic and practical. His latest book is a great toolbox for leaders living on the cutting edge."

Walt Kallestad, pastor, Community Church of Joy ELCA (now Dream City Church), Glendale, Arizona

Select Books by the Authors

Carl F. George with Warren Bird

The Coming Church Revolution:
Empowering Leaders for the Future (Revell, 1994)

Carl F. George with Warren Bird

Prepare Your Church for the Future (Revell, 1991)

Carl F. George and Robert E. Logan

Leading and Managing Your Church (Revell, 1987)

William Vanderbloemen and Warren Bird

Next: Pastoral Succession That Works (Baker, 2014)

(see bibliography for additional author titles)

HOW TO
BREAK
GROWTH
BARRIERS

REVISE YOUR ROLE, RELEASE YOUR PEOPLE, AND CAPTURE OVERLOOKED OPPORTUNITIES FOR YOUR CHURCH

UPDATED EDITION

CARL F. GEORGE
AND WARREN BIRD

BakerBooks

a division of Baker Publishing Group
Grand Rapids, Michigan

Published by Baker Books
a division of Baker Publishing Group
P.O. Box 6287, Grand Rapids, MI 49516-6287
www.bakerbooks.com

Printed in the United States of America

Library of Congress Cataloging-in-Publication Data is on file at the Library of Congress, Washington, DC.

978-0-8010-9246-6

Illustrations by David Rodriguez, www.drgorilla.com. Used by permission.

17 18 19 20 21 22 23   7 6 5 4 3 2

Contents

List of Figures

Preface

My (Carl George) formal church ministry began as an intern in a church that had broken the 1,000 barrier. This church was startlingly different from every church I had known. Not only did they keep breaking records at every level—baptisms, conversions, numbers of trained leaders, and overall attendance—but I quickly recognized that this church took a different approach than what I had previously seen or experienced.

During that era, there were growing churches, stable churches, and dying churches, just like today. Some were new and others long established, again like today. But I came to realize within each of these types of churches a few leaders were bringing a new notion of what the church could be. They began kicking out the walls—both figuratively and literally—imagining that their church could and should achieve a greater harvest of people. As they asked, "*Why* aren't we beyond _____?" [200, 400, 800, or whatever level they were at], they also began to dream, "And what would it be like to *take* a church there?"

This book tells the story of the transitions behind breaking those barriers. It unwraps both the how and the why. And it presses you, the reader, to make certain decisions both about your own leadership health and about inquiring whether God wants to entrust more souls into your church's care.

How to Break Growth Barriers will also ask you to take stock of your current ministry: Are you leading leaders? What would happen at your church if you developed and empowered *more* leaders? Not only would your role change but your congregation would as well. Very likely, it would grow and break new growth barriers. Then you'd need even more leaders and more spiritual caregivers!

Does Your Church Need More Shepherds?

This book is for church leaders who are committed to leading by example but also want to have a greater impact as they do so. You want to do more than personally model the roles of spiritual leadership and caregiving; you also want to lead *more people* at your church to do so, and ultimately to lead other *leaders* especially to develop yet more leaders.

If you follow the principles in this book, the prognosis for growth in almost any church will be greatly improved. In addition, the prognosis for your own emotional health will be strong as well.

Does it seem overly bold or even inappropriate to make claims that big? We believe those outcomes are what Scripture teaches. We've also seen the principles work in a wide variety of contexts over the last thirty years.

How to Break Growth Barriers is much more than theory. Buckle up, because you are about to go on a ministry-transforming ride.

Origins of the Book

This book is actually an updated version of a volume by the same title originally released in 1993 that traces its origin to an extremely popular series of conferences that Carl George developed, often serving as one of the speakers. Warren Bird often served as the emcee. Along the way Warren conducted a research project on conference alumni, learning that they gave the conference content very high marks in helping them actually break through various growth barriers. At that point, Warren asked if he could combine the best of each conference into a book.

That original book sold so well, continuing to do so year after year, that the publisher has asked us to update it for a new generation. For this edition, every single paragraph has been revised and updated in some way. The core ideas and outline remain unchanged, but both the art and the illustrations have been reframed for today.

In this edition, as well as the original, the "I" voice across the book is that of Carl George. Coauthor Warren Bird and I have worked together for a long time. Sometimes our views are so compatible that we sound more like a solo than a duet. When I speak of an idea, it may actually have been mine, but after he edits it I often prefer how it turns out, and I find myself unable to distinguish what part was his and what was mine. He lets me take credit for the concepts, but I very much admire how he positions the ideas for publication.

Ready?

One of the themes you'll encounter throughout the book is this: Do you believe an enormous potential for spiritual harvest is at your church's doorstep? If your answer is yes—or if you hope to discover that the answer is yes—then please proceed.

PART 1

IDENTIFY YOUR VISION

What Can This Book Do for You?

Go with me to a country just hit by a devastating earthquake, where fifty thousand people are injured or dead. Two almost identical medical teams, each headed by a doctor, are being airlifted into the heart of the disaster area.

The physician leading the first crew steps out of the helicopter and is immediately overwhelmed by all the carnage. There, barely ten paces away, workers are pulling a mangled but living body from under the rubble.

Moved by compassion, the doctor rushes over and calculates the personnel, equipment, and facilities needed to help this victim. He assigns half his medical team and half their supplies to work on this one person.

A handful of survivors, sensing the availability of help, bring the physician another case. This victim is in even worse condition. The doctor assigns the rest of his medical team and resources to care for this person.

Now the doctor faces a worse dilemma than when his helicopter touched down. He would like to treat 49,998 more people but has already expended virtually all his resources on the first two bodies presented to him.

The only solution, he decides, is to make himself even more available. He resolves that he and his staff will push themselves harder. They will be on call twenty hours a day, seven days a week, to treat as many individuals as possible.

Unfortunately, a few weeks later this well-intentioned medic is forced to return home. His body has not been able to keep pace with his desire to help. With his resistance lowered, he has caught one of the diseases rampant in the disaster area. The care he and his team have provided must come to a standstill until his replacement arrives.

Meanwhile, what is the second medical team doing? Their preliminary assessment, likewise, takes only a matter of moments. They, too, are deeply shocked and moved with compassion toward the massive death and pain evident in every direction. They see widespread malnutrition, open wounds, and other horrible conditions.

People are suffering and dying before their eyes.

The physician heading this second unit quickly concludes that her small group by itself is inadequate. So instead of scooping up the first person in sight and immediately beginning treatment, this doctor opts for a different plan. She tries to calculate a strategy that will touch a maximum number of people in the least amount of time, using the scarce resources available.

The doctor announces to her team, "Let's train some people as life-support engineers." One group will make sure safe drinking water is available, another will deal with shelter issues, and another with food. Yet another group will work on waste control and public health by repairing the citywide sewer system to take the fecal matter off the streets before it mixes into the water supply or spreads into the homes.

This relief and preventative care, multiplied throughout the disaster area, will retard the growth of infection and allow the medical intervention to have a greater impact.

Having mapped out a program to provide the essentials of survival and reduce infectious agents, the doctor next addresses issues of proper nutrition and other preventable forms of need.

In the meantime, her medical team begins training the healthier survivors to serve as health officers. Their focus is on remedial and interventional care, starting with the people who, if treated, have a good prognosis for recovery.

Everyone in the disaster area is keenly aware that a very practical reason exists for giving priority to those who are getting well. The need is of such tremendous proportions that every additional able-bodied worker can help make a significant difference.

Which Team Would You Choose?

Suppose you, as a typical North American pastor or Christian leader, were to watch the above-described scenario and be asked which of the medical teams was more *caring*. Which would you choose? Remember, both teams had equally strong feelings of love and compassion. They differed only in how they showed their concern.

The initial response of most Christians, including trained leaders, is to choose to act like the first group. They want to help, their willingness to personally do whatever it takes plunges them into immediate action, and their compassion focuses their attention on the most urgent needs.

However, I suggest and will affirm this underlying principle throughout this book: an emphasis on leadership development as illustrated by the second group above paves the way for a higher level of long-range care. A systems-based approach of empowering others, when prayerfully operated in dependence on the Holy Spirit, is the most effective way to deliver the most widespread continuing infusion of desperately needed care. It also models most closely the way Jesus worked with His twelve disciples.

Unfortunately, like the first doctor in this example, many of us fail to recognize what can happen when a crisis is of such tremendous scope. The field of need is too big for us. We frantically work twenty hours a day, only to come down with spiritual chronic fatigue syndrome. Worse, our underlying motivation will stem from a mistaken assumption: we wrongly suppose that the key to effective ministry is our personal availability.

That is, most pastors frame their priorities around an inaccurate supposition that widespread ministry will occur only when they are active as primary caregivers.

I propose this alternative: the more fundamental need is for church leaders to craft a systemic approach to pastoral care.[1] To the extent that caregivers in a local church become so preoccupied with the nearest bleeding body that they cannot keep the whole system alive, they will allow whole sections of their church to perish in the process.[2] They must, rather, attend to the big picture.

> We wrongly suppose that the key to effective ministry is our personal availability.

Pastors and lay leaders must see with eyes of faith to catch a glimpse of a bigger view of their church's ministry. They cannot continue to accept the first case to cross their path, wrap their lives around it, and allow the rest of the world to go down the tubes. Rather, church leaders must allocate their resources as strategically as a medical emergency team triages a crisis. They do not demonstrate wise leadership if they provide all the ministry themselves, even if they do discover how to clock in a twenty-five-hour day.

Too many people's lives are broken or devastated. They need continuing large doses of prayer, ongoing care, and special attention. The church will want to try to make sure the help they need is available to them.

But other people require just a little assistance, and then they can help with the ministering.

Yes, it is heartrending to bypass one needy person to give attention to another. Yes, such choices will receive recriminations by certain well-intentioned church people. But church leaders who want to maximize their impact through other capable (and trainable) workers must develop a new means of budgeting their energies.

Remember, however, the need on which this master plan is built. In no way does it stem from a lack of mercy. Rather, the leader's prayerful goal is to determine how to apply his or her time and energy so that the most people can receive the best possible care in the shortest amount of time with the best use of the resources.

> *Church leaders must allocate their resources as strategically as a medical emergency team triages a crisis.*

Ultimately this multiplication strategy, when guided and empowered by the Holy Spirit, will result in the most people being touched. In addition, sometimes a leader's best personal growth occurs while he or she learns to train others for leadership.

Why This Book Is Relevant to You

This book is designed to help you, a church leader, enlarge your vision for what God wants to do through your church. It will also coach you in the leadership perspective and skills necessary to break through whatever current growth barrier you face.

To begin, chapters 2 and 3 will help you identify the vision God has for your church, as well as the vision you currently convey to your people. You will also gain insight into how to develop a more listening-sensitive life and how to increase your "visionizing" abilities.

Chapter 4 will help you see your church as a system so as to better discern if its current care structure is fostering or squelching growth. You will finish this chapter with a better handle on the importance of accurately diagnosing your particular church situation.

Chapter 5 deals with motive: Why should you want your church to grow? What are some unhealthy factors that can lie behind a growth momentum? Does God necessarily call every church to numerical growth?

The heart of the book, chapters 6 and 7, contrasts the ministry coach and solo caregiver styles of ministry, explains why the solo caregiver mentality is usually a fundamental obstacle to most church growth and health, and offers you guidance to assess your leadership gifts and style.

Then come several illustrations of what the role of coaching could look like in your ministry (chapter 8), especially as it relates to certain conflicts in the church. You will also understand how the codependency and recovery movement is linked to the solo caregiver's dilemma (chapter 9).

The rest of the book shows how to break specific growth barriers. What are the keys to breaking the 200 barrier (chapter 10), the 400 barrier (chapter 11), and the 800 barrier (chapter 12)? These are not numerical barriers so much as general sizes when certain patterns and scales need to change if a church is to meaningfully care for more souls.

The final chapter (chapter 13) points you to the ministry paradigm of the future. It explains why certain churches experience phenomenal conversion growth and wholehearted discipleship. It shows how to build these essential components into your church right now so as to lay the foundation for unimpeded growth in the future.

Maybe Your Situation Is Different

Whatever size church you now serve, chances are that numerous growth opportunities are present but overlooked. After a career of consulting across dozens of denominations, I have yet to be in a church where more growth opportunity is not present than the church is willing to respond to.

Church growth is like planted grass. If you stand on the seeded bed, the new green shoots do not have a chance. But give them water and light, and they will grow naturally in most cases.

Does that analogy seem too simplistic? I believe it describes what God wants to do for His church. He wants to build it in such a way that not even the gates of hell can block its expansion (Matt. 16:18).

I have yet to be in a church where more growth opportunity is not present than the church is willing to respond to.

Could it be that we are so accustomed to working with bonsai trees that we have lost sight of and hope for ongoing, unstunted growth? Could we church leaders, like a dynasty of gardeners, be part of an ongoing tradition that twists, bruises, pinches, and clips the roots of our churches so as to prevent their being overtaken by growth? Maybe, despite our intentions otherwise, we do so without even realizing it.

Barriers to growth can usually be resolved. The key issue at your church is probably not a stubborn deacon or even a perennially unmet church budget. Instead, it is probably the lack of a workable set of values to overcome certain obstacles in ministry. This looks like a clear case of "We have met the enemy, and he is us."

The first people to deal with in the chain of change are the ministers, because they set a pace that either assures nongrowth or permits growth.

Are You a Solo Caregiver or a Ministry Coach?

As with the medical teams described earlier, the needs around you are of such tremendous proportions that all systems of care can be completely overwhelmed. Hurting people are in such abundance that they can almost drive you to sleeplessness.

The typical response to widespread need is what this book will call *solo caregiving*. This style of caring makes the pastor available as the primary caregiver to everyone who will respond.

By contrast, just as the more realistic and practical scenario for the second doctor in the earthquake zone was to teach people mutual self-care, you, too, must attend to the management dimension. This style of caring is what I will call *coaching*.[3]

To become a ministry coach you learn to do more than offer empathetic responses to human need. You also acknowledge certain realities, such as knowing *you* cannot deliver help to all people at the levels they require. Instead, you must take a more empowering and conceptual view of things (as explained in chapters 6 through 9), which in the long run is not only most loving but is the perspective Jesus exemplified.

In short, I suggest a changed paradigm for church leadership. You must shift from trying to do all the caring, which often means you do it yourself, to seeing to it that people get cared for, which means you develop and manage a system of caregiving that will include as many of your church's lay leaders as possible (see Figure 1, p. 29).

The principles in this book do not require that you abandon your caregiving skills. You will model giving care so your skills will be used with double effect. Follow these principles and adopt a new perspective on shepherding, one that shepherds other shepherds in your congregation, and you will enable an entire ranch to be shepherded. You will learn to whom you should make yourself available as a primary caregiver and how you can best allocate the time and energy you put into hands-on ministry.

This rancher outlook (which this book often calls a caregiving coach) is taught by a number of leadership mentors. Although their terminology may vary, a unifying theme runs through each of the following:

Growth barriers are usually broken when the pastor dreams a bigger dream. . . . The problem with most pastors is that they don't dream big enough. . . . What you have to do is allow it to grow by giving it the right environment. . . . Your church is not going to go to the next level until you do.

Bill Easum and Bill Cornelius,
Go Big: Lead Your Church to Explosive Growth[4]

Growth, evangelism and the expansion of the church depend as much on a leader's ability to develop an expansive infrastructure as on any other factor except prayer. . . . The church that grows beyond the 200 barrier is the church that decides to minister to its people in a comprehensive organization rather than a family-type fellowship.

Bill M. Sullivan,
Ten Steps to Breaking the 200 Barrier[5]

Church growth cannot be sustained unless the laity are mobilized to fulfill their distinctive ministries both in the church and in the world. . . .

In a small church of up to say 65, the management style of the leader will probably be at the level of foreman. . . . He is available to be personally involved in every task which comes to hand.

In churches with a membership of between 66 and 150, the most frequently encountered leadership level is that of supervisor. . . . He is on hand to deal with an emergency and resolve any difficulties which may arise. Church ministers who operate in this way have their phones constantly ringing, or find people forever at the door. . . . The leader has to change his management style to middle management level to get far into the 151–450 member bracket. Middle management involves delegation with accountability. When people are invited to undertake some responsibilities in the church, they are given appropriate decision-making power. . . .

The church with more than 450 members . . . needs top-level management skills to weld his professional team together. . . .

When a church tops the 1,000 membership mark . . . the presiding minister . . . functions as chairman of the board. He dreams his dreams, formulates his plans, and excites others with the vision of his perceptions of where the church could be five years hence.

Eddie Gibbs,
I Believe in Church Growth[6]

There is very persuasive evidence that suggests that: (1) the normal historical pressures on the pastor, especially in smaller congregations and in new missions, tend to cause him to accept a shepherd role; (2) if the pastor of a new mission accepts the shepherd role in the early years of the new mission, attendance probably will level off at an average of less than one hundred . . . ; (3) the churches that continue to increase in size year after year tend to have rancher-style ministers as their pastors; (4) small congregations and many of the congregations that are declining in size tend to have shepherd-style pastors; and (5) after a congregation has experienced being served by a shepherd-style minister the members often resist, oppose, or resent a minister who seeks to function in a rancher-style role.

In simple language it appears that one reason approximately one-half of all the congregations in American Protestantism average fewer than 75 at the principal weekly worship service is the combination of the traditional image of the role of the pastor with the normal institutional and personal pressures that cause the minister to function as a shepherd. . . . The shepherd role . . . tends to inhibit the evangelistic outreach of those congregations.

Lyle E. Schaller,
Survival Tactics in the Parish[7]

Two leadership style shifts are required for breaking the "125 Barrier." Shift #1: The pastor must shift from establishing deep one-to-one relationships to establishing group relationship. . . . Shift #2: The pastor must shift from being a foreman to being a supervisor. An effective supervisor delegates responsibility. . . . Growing past the "125 barrier" requires a shift from "doing it all yourself" to "getting others involved."

Harry H. Fowler,
Breaking Barriers of New Church Growth[8]

Figure 1

Are You a *Lone* Caregiver?

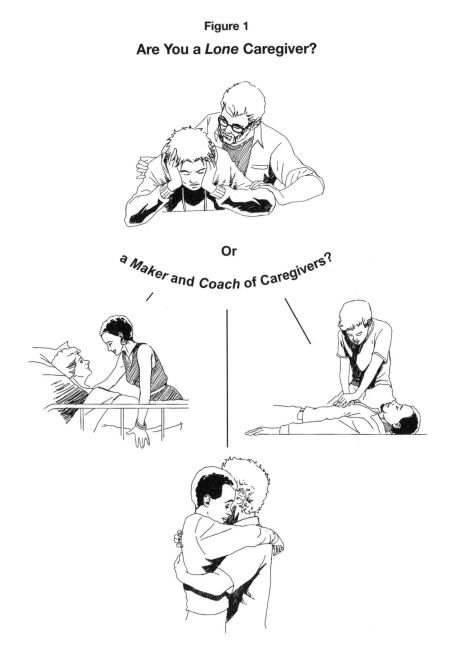

Or

a *Maker* and *Coach* of Caregivers?

29

The most formidable obstacle to growth that I know of is a pastor who thinks negatively and who is pessimistic about growth opportunities in the community. Such a pastor generally feels that the basic task of the church is to care for those sheep already in the fold rather than to concentrate on winning lost sheep and constantly incorporating new ones into the flock. . . .

If the first vital sign of a growing church is a pastor who is using God-given gifts to lead the church into growth, the second is a well-mobilized laity. . . .

In a smaller church of up to 200 members the pastor can do all the work, and many do. But such a church will not be able to grow past that point without lay ministry.

Pastors of growing churches, whether they be large or small, know how to motivate their laypeople, how to create structures which permit them to be active and productive, and how to guide them into meaningful avenues of Christian service.

Peter Wagner,
Your Church Can Grow[9]

No church can grow beyond the ability of the pastoral leader to delegate responsibilities to staff and lay ministers. . . . Lay ministers must become a mobilized force in the church if significant growth is to occur. . . . The pastor in a growing church is always a central figure, but he is careful to surround himself with gifted, responsible, work-oriented laypersons who function as lay ministers.

Charles Chaney and Ron Lewis,
Design for Church Growth[10]

What got your church to where it is will not get it to where you want it to be. . . . Larger churches are not just bigger versions of smaller churches; in reality they are an entirely different entity that requires different operational procedures.

Gary L. McIntosh,
*Taking Your Church to the Next Level:
What Got You Here Won't Get You There*[11]

Just how many sheep can one shepherd know, feed, love, protect, and direct? New Testament evidence abounds that a plurality of elders existed in cities where churches were established. . . . If properly decentralized . . . lay ministers are considered the "nervous system" of the church. They show concern to the families of the church and serve as a communication line concerning illness, bereavement, and joyful occasions among the members. They also seek to encourage each member to participate fully in the church's programs. Among many churches this practical implementation of the "shepherd-sheep" concept is taking on a greater importance.

Elmer Towns, John Vaughan, and David Seifert,
The Complete Book of Church Growth[12]

Do you see the common thread in what these growth specialists all say? Effective leaders accomplish the work through others. The task is too great for one person. It is more important for the leader of a growing church to produce other leaders than to perform personal ministry. The irony is that caring ministry is always better modeled than assigned. It is not a question of either/or ("shall they care or should I care?") but rather of both/and ("when I demonstrate care, they can care better by following my example").

> *Effective leaders accomplish the work through others. The task is too great for one person.*

All pastors and lay leaders who grasp this concept and act on it will find the scope of their ministry broadened. Many may gain insight into certain long-standing patterns of personal codependency (to be discussed in chapter 9). Still others will discover a delightful liberation from the "oughts" of false guilt.

The ideas in this book, which I believe are both grounded in Scripture and sensitive to what the Holy Spirit wants to do in our time, are tools that will help us evangelize and disciple our cities and towns beyond our wildest imaginations. Follow-up gaps will be filled.

Alienation and despair will be transformed into hope, faith, and love. And broken families will be rebuilt as people are reparented in the context of spiritual kinship groups.

My hope also is that readers will understand why Jesus urges them to focus their prayers not merely on the harvest nor on themselves as ministers but on the leadership-formation issue: that the Lord of the harvest will "send out workers into his harvest field" (Matt. 9:38).

Are you ready for such a challenge?

FOR FURTHER THOUGHT

1. Of the two medical team leaders described, whose vision and management style is most similar to yours? Where does the analogy break down in your situation?

2. In your church experience, would you say the coaching style or the solo caregiver style is more predominant? Why? What factors influence churches to desire shepherds who do all the caring themselves versus those who develop other caregivers?

3. What is the main purpose and message of this book? Which chapter appears to be most relevant for you?

4. Of the different writers quoted in this chapter, who spoke most pointedly to you?

5. Based on your knowledge of Scripture, what teachings and illustrations come to mind that support a solo caregiver perspective of leadership? A coach perspective?

6. Put check marks in front of your three areas of greatest strength. Put asterisks in front of the three that probably need the most improvement.

   ☐ Knowing God's vision for your church (ch. 2).

   ☐ Communicating vision to your church (ch. 3).

☐ Detecting vision limiters in your church (ch. 2).

☐ Practicing a prayer life that is open to vision (ch. 2).

☐ Understanding the sources of growth in your church (ch. 4).

☐ Being willing to ask God if He has a greater agenda for your church than you do (ch. 5).

☐ Viewing the coaching ministry style as a more effective disciple-making strategy than the solo caregiver style (ch. 6).

☐ Identifying ways that you behave like a solo caregiver (chs. 6 and 7).

☐ Identifying ways that you behave like a coach to others (chs. 6 and 7).

☐ Dealing with difficult groups in your church (ch. 8).

☐ Understanding how your upbringing and personal co-dependencies affect your ministry (chs. 8 and 9).

☐ Developing a specific strategy to break current numeric growth barriers (chs. 10, 11, and 12).

☐ Developing a long-range plan designed to prevent your church from becoming less caring as it grows larger (ch. 13).

How Can You Enlarge Your Vision?

After King David led Israel into an era of unprecedented peace, security, and wealth, he held a conversation with the prophet Nathan, which I paraphrase from 2 Samuel 7.

"How do you like my new cedar-lined, state-of-the-art king's mansion?" David asked.

"Pretty nice," came Nathan's reply.

"I've been thinking about building one for God," David commented.

"Great idea. Do what's in your heart," answered Nathan.

But that night the Lord said to Nathan, "Go tell David I didn't ask for that. I'm in the business of providing houses for *him*. When did I ask him to make a home for *Me*? All I want David to do is to be My servant."

The implication? It is easy to create a dream of what we could do for God without consulting Him to ask what He has in mind. Just because we have thought up an idea and can list ways it could bring glory to our Lord does not mean we have any guarantee that He has said yes.

What leaders sometimes find confusing is the role that creative imagination has in forming a ministry vision. Without discernment, whatever a leader visualizes can be mislabeled as a heaven-sent vision. The prophet Jeremiah warned of this when he contrasted human dreams with revelation from heaven (Jer. 23:28).

The purpose of this chapter and the next, therefore, is to offer guidance in identifying the vision God has for your church as well as the vision that guides you at present. You will also gain insight into how to increase your vision-casting or communicating abilities and how to develop a more listening-sensitive prayer life.

What Can Vision Do?

Your ability to provide leadership to your church is directly connected to how you envision a preferred future and then effectively communicate that goal to your constituency.

Today's business world, for example, was enhanced by the vision of a man named Fred Smith. He conceived of a way to make geography irrelevant. He said, in effect, "We're going to fix it so that if Joe or Susie Customer orders a widget, we can make it possible to have that widget on their desk the next morning by 10:00, no matter where in North America they live."

Today services like Amazon Prime have carried it a step further, but companies had to design an entire system of tools, from airplane fleets to state-of-the-art computerized inventory control, to make Fred's words true. Meanwhile I can track the pathway of my package in real time. This all happens not by accident but because someone prepared and executed a vision.

What Can Limit Your Vision?

I regularly listen to pastors and lay leaders as they talk about their dreams and goals. Most of them already have some kind of vision they can articulate. But in their accounts I often detect the equivalent of signposts on the highways of their imaginations. These markers, because of the restrictions they create, virtually guarantee that most churches will not achieve their full potential.

What does that mental image say? "Vision Limit, Do Not Exceed."

This chapter will help you identify those markers that may at first appear to identify full-fledged visions but in reality have their own built-in limitations on visions of growth. It will also show you how to ask God if He has a greater agenda for your church than you do.

I have counted at least fifteen such limiting vision shapers. Each of them restrains a pastor's leadership ability and a church's growth and health.

1. Focus on fixing what breaks.

The first vision limiter stems from a problem-solving focus. Peter Drucker, author of such books as *Managing the Non-Profit Organization*, insists that problem solving is an important aspect of management. He points out, however, that the primary accomplishment of problem solving is to take something that is unraveled and reweave it so that it works just about as well as it did before it broke. But, Drucker says, mere problem solving fails to capitalize on emerging opportunity.[1]

Therefore, a problem-solving focus will not necessarily guide a church to grow significantly. Instead, it is more likely to help a church merely maintain its present circumstances.

Someone has said that church leaders have become keepers of the aquarium rather than fishermen of the deep. Tending the aquarium (or the flock) is an important role. No one should downplay its significance. At the same time, remember that doing so does not automatically lead to reaching more people.

In most situations, unless evangelism is present, growth cannot be sustained.

True, in some cases where a strong birthrate is present, a problem-solving focus assists a church in preserving what it has and even enlarging as a result. But in most situations, unless evangelism is present, growth cannot be sustained.

2. Working to our full capacity and then some.

A second growth limiter occurs when a church's leadership says, "I'm busy enough now." When translated, those words usually mean, "I feel tired, and my vision of a 'preferred future' is to be less tired. If I'm this weary now, what am I going to feel like if we add a 10 percent increase to every ministry I now oversee?"

I discovered this full-calendar limit as I watched one pastor personally sign seven hundred letters for his parish's annual fund campaign. When he had done around three hundred, he looked over at me, stopped only long enough to turn the page for the next signature, and said, "With seven hundred people on my roll, I have all I can say grace over now. If you're asking me for money to help start a new work, I will gladly put it in the budget for which I am signing these letters, but please don't ask me to accept more sheep in the flock. The ones I have now are just about getting away from me."

He did possess a vision of sorts. It was to watch out for his sheep well enough so that he could live and they would feel adequately managed. There is nothing inherently wrong with these results—if the Almighty has called him to do just that much, and no more.

3. Keeping pace with other churches.

Third, some people follow a lockstep vision limit. This barrier to an enlarged harvest says, "I must make certain not to go any more slowly than my colleagues are going." In other words, "My standard is to keep up with the rest of the pack."

If you are such a leader, you are begging for fatigue. Why? Opportunities vary from church to church. The mix and fit between your personality, your time of life, the maturity level of the church you now serve, and so forth, may sharply contrast with that of your sister church across town.

Maybe their mortgage was paid off by a timely bequest and yours was not (or vice versa). Maybe their pastoral family, with their 2.4

children, is at the perfect age and life stage for that church and yours does not seem to be (or vice versa).

The lockstep mentality does reflect a vision of sorts. And it can drive a church's behavior. "Well, Pastor, *they're* having a successful vacation Bible school. Just look at the banners when you drive by their building. Why can't we have a successful vacation Bible school?" Sometimes it works because it promotes action through envy.

The lockstep pattern can work in reverse as well. If you break step and shoot upward like a sunflower in a garden of poppies, your "friends" may want to prune you back. If your church grows and receives attention at more than one annual denominational meeting in a row, you might be abandoned by people who were once pleasant to be around. Some of them will be caught up in jealousy and will challenge your motives, shun you, and otherwise criticize you.

In short, for you to compare yourself with the "average" church, whether it leads to your grumbling or gloating, is unproductive. Doing so will tie you into a lockstep pattern that says, "We've got to do better, because I do not want to be asked by my spouse or colleagues why we're not keeping up."

4. Making budget.

Fourth, some churches are driven by a vision to grow because they know their survival is at stake. They are motivated to pay their bills, so the extent of their vision is in direct proportion to the size of their bills.

Unfortunately, some pastors and churches address this issue by adjusting the break-even point downward. After all, since more than half the expenses of a typical church go toward staff support, then the less money a pastor needs from the church, the smaller size the church can be. Pastoral spouses who work outside the church, second jobs for the pastor, generous relatives, outside donors, and other factors can be used to ensure that the ministerial family poses the most minimal drain possible on the church budget.

If abundant funding does come in, what happens to the vision? For example, suppose a windfall (something you receive as a result of something you do not do) comes your way from the bequest of a well-to-do member who died. This favorable turn of finances does not necessarily remove the limiting survival vision. Instead, it usually demotivates leadership. There is no longer a reason to keep pushing. "We do not have to get out in the fray of battle anymore, so we will take it easy for a while." A church with a sizable endowment account is almost impossible to motivate to grow.

Or what if the church does indeed grow and is able to pay its pastoral staff more; will that solve the survival limiter? In other words, will an increased pastoral standard of living affect the motivation for growing a church? Probably not. But, given how most pastors are compensated, I rarely advise them to turn down the pay raise.[2]

5. Becoming stable and secure.

I call the fifth vision limiter the goal of a generic stand-alone church. In many suburban people's imagination, the ideal church has its own building, presumably painted white with a small steeple, in a comfortable suburb with shade trees over the parking lot. In urban settings, it's in a neighborhood that's both safe and growing, with an attractive facility in good repair. It supports one full-time pastor who can give his wife the opportunity to be a full-time homemaker and can send their children through college. It has no need to enlarge the church facility.

This pastor has a part-time administrative assistant, a part-time custodian, and a part-time youth or worship leader—not enough staff to require using management skills, but enough that the nitty-gritty is done by others. Sunday school literature seems written primarily for this idyllic situation.

For many pastors and board members, this vision of a stand-alone church is enough to cause them to reach beyond where they are. Am I criticizing such a church or lifestyle? No. Any light at all that causes you to see a preferred future condition is preferable to no light.

My encouragement is to continue forward, because this vision—like most others—is going to run out at a point that may be short of what God intends.

6. Stretching just slightly.

Growth limiter number six involves comfort. This view is conveyed by words like, "If there were only one thousand dollars more in the budget, or just three or four more volunteers, then everything would be just fine."

To detect situations like these, you ask a pastor or church board, "What would you like to see happen here?" If they answer, "Perhaps be 10 percent larger than we are now, so we would be in a more comfortable position," then you can predict that the church will stretch itself for about a year. Such a goal offers an incentive of sorts, but what if God has a greater scope of ministry in mind?

7. Putting a cap on "enough."

Next comes the "No Vacancy" sign. Have you driven by a family-run motel and seen a neon light that read, "Sorry, No Vacancy"? Motel managers have a switch inside their office which they activate when the bed level is full enough.

In tight-cash times the switch is not touched until 1:00 a.m., when every room is rented, including the one with the broken TV. In good times, if it is 9:00 p.m. and the proprietors are tired, they flip the switch.

Some churches have a similar system, and they activate the "No Vacancy" indicator at the earliest opportunity possible. If the parking lot is full, or the sanctuary is full, or the Sunday schools are full, do you do anything about it, or just enjoy it? Another somewhat comical way of visualizing this limiter is to watch a fisherman throw back fish he deems too large for his skillet. He sets out with a notion about how far he is willing to go.

8. *Circling the wagons to remain safe.*

The eighth vision limiter is a fortress mentality in which the wagons are drawn in a circle. I grew up in a very conservative group where some taught that we were the only true churches left. If only we had eyes to see from a satellite, we would have realized that the ecclesiastical landscape was filled with scores of denominations of our size and type doing likewise: pulling their wagons together in a very tight circle. Somehow, all of us were the only ones left.

Even so, that climate helped build a fierce sense of morale. Our vision of how right we were produced the strength of camaraderie. It got us out of bed and propelled activity. But it did not necessarily provide the loving context into which others could find acceptance.

9. *Raising and supporting homegrown missionaries.*

I once heard a pastor say, "I have a vision that God will call people from this church to the mission field. It is my intention to stay here and grow this church, so that we have enough giving ability to support every missionary God calls from this church."

My initial impression was, "That sounds like a great goal." His church had commissioned 140 missionaries, and he had built a church of two thousand persons to make good on that pledge.

That seemed to be an appropriate vision for him. The problem is that most churches can look back over fifty years of no one entering pastoral ministry or missionary service. Thus, with no one to support, they have no incentive to grow.

10. *Developing a paid-staff role for each child.*

The tenth vision limiter is the idea of a family staff—a job for all the children as they enter adulthood. If the pastoral couple had nine or ten kids, this vision would give them a high standard to shoot for. But what happens after they have involved all their children plus their spouses? And what about the one- or two-child pastoral family?

11. Restoring the church's golden era.

In some cases, a more blunt description is that of recovering ghosts. The matriarchs and patriarchs of the church can walk through the sanctuary and find people in every empty pew. "That's the Pettits' pew," they will say. If I ask where they are, I am told, "Oh, they moved to Indiana years ago." Same with the Edwardses who, except for their oldest son, are now in Maryland, and Pam Maas who moved her membership to the church across town six years ago, and the Bartels who were railroaded out of the church by a powerful elder, whose son is head elder today.

These people might come back for a homecoming event or when in town over the holidays, but trying to produce attendance growth from them can be like giving blood to a leukemia victim. If you fail to do something about the bone marrow, you must keep pumping in transfusions.

The idea of building bridges with former members is not wrong. It does reflect a form of vision. It drives some ministry. It may not be all God has in mind, however.

You can invest enormous amounts of energy trying to reach disillusioned or lapsed members, but the old wounds are very hard to heal. As Lyle Schaller and others have pointed out, it is probably two or three times more fruitful to go after unsolicited contacts than to attempt to raise the dead.[3]

Many churches will point to thirty-year-old photographs on the wall that depict a packed-out sanctuary or Sunday school big event. Longtime members will lament, "If we can only rebuild what we had back then."

When I examine the photo I usually see all Anglo faces. Then I go outside and see nothing but African American, Hispanic, or Asian faces, and I comment, "We'd have to recolor that photograph for it ever to happen here again." Unfortunately, that often silences them, because their vision of reenacting the past does not allow for any ethnic transition.

12. Closing the back doors.

This approach may range from keeping the young people from dropping out to raising the church's visitor-retention ratio. It most often falls into a problem-solving mentality that reduces falling away, such as when a popular and effective youth leader moves away and must be replaced quickly or see the group suffer a sharp decline in morale. But discerning leaders will recognize that befriended people do not readily give up relationships in which they are satisfyingly engaged, so will give much energy to helping newcomers get acquainted. Inward focus may stabilize a congregation, but eventually a new source of prospective members must be identified and pursued. It's who is not here yet that counts in the long term!

> *A new source of prospective members must be identified and pursued. It's who is not here yet that counts in the long term!*

13. Creating temporary surges without follow-up.

Thirteenth is the rally or high-visibility event. "Let's sponsor a concert series," someone will say. Or, "Let's have an annual homecoming and get some action going around here." This approach, which rallies the church and boosts morale, too often produces results that last for only a few weeks. It may momentarily fill the hall, revival style, without regard to whether there is a durable structure underneath. It produces more of an audience than a spiritually connected congregation.

14. Establishing a mesa-culture mentality.

This attitude says, "We will reach all who can climb to where we are and meet our standards." When these words are translated into denominational terms, it means that the majority of persons in the outside community cannot qualify.

43

Such groups might vigorously affirm that the gospel is for all people but at the same time they create subtle entrance requirements, usually of an ethnic nature, that exclude the majority of the surrounding community.

For example, in certain Lutheran churches, the only way to be accepted is to be the child of a German immigrant, or to marry the child of a parishioner, or to have been a foreign exchange student who studied in Germany. Short of that, getting in is very difficult, typically requiring an in-marriage and a generation or so. As a result, the outflow is often greater than the inflow.

15. Resting on an already fulfilled or outgrown vision.

Many a preacher-leader has built the largest facility or attendance in town. Such leaders have touched what they knew of need in the community but then lost their vision because nothing new replaced it. If they fail to seek the Lord for fresh direction, or if through the work of the enemy they become distracted or preoccupied by some intervening mess, they will plateau, rest on their laurels, or even stagnate.

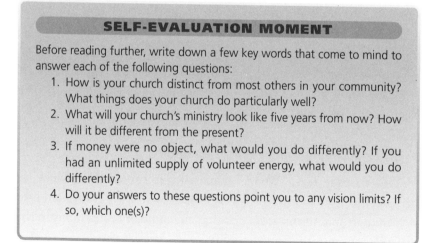

SELF-EVALUATION MOMENT

Before reading further, write down a few key words that come to mind to answer each of the following questions:
1. How is your church distinct from most others in your community? What things does your church do particularly well?
2. What will your church's ministry look like five years from now? How will it be different from the present?
3. If money were no object, what would you do differently? If you had an unlimited supply of volunteer energy, what would you do differently?
4. Do your answers to these questions point you to any vision limits? If so, which one(s)?

A Vision You Will Not Outgrow

Is there a goal more durable than the fifteen listed above? Will every vision ultimately prove to be inadequate?

Not that anything is inherently wrong with these objectives, limiting as they become. True, sometimes people ask, "What went wrong with our vision?" and the real culprit was a church fight or moral failure. But those distractions can be dealt with, usually on one's knees.

Each factor I have listed is indeed a form of vision. It does inform activity and guide behavior. It focuses people and causes them to cooperate. Each opens the door for a certain growth potential. But, like the governor on a carburetor, it slows you down at a certain point. It may carry you from this week to the next week but will probably not take you to one year, three years, or five years from now.

I propose a dream so enduring that it has yet to be fulfilled. Those who pursue it live with an ongoing resolution in their hearts that they will make a difference in ministry.

This vision-influencing factor, the only one that seems limitless, is to view the thousands of people around you as a harvest field. (I will further describe this limitless harvest in chapter 12.) It comes from Jesus's words to His disciples: "Open your eyes and look at the fields! They are ripe for harvest. Even now the one who reaps draws a wage and harvests a crop for eternal life. . . . Others have done the hard work, and you have reaped the benefits of their labor" (John 4:35–36, 38). The contrast between this harvest vision and a limited vision is highlighted in Figure 2 below.

Before you entered the mission field represented by your church, God went first. Before you arrived there, He had already sowed. The prayers of parents, the gospel preaching of others, and the witness of Christians before you have all been used by God to prepare a harvest.

This means that people are ready to respond to Christ, waiting for whichever representative of Jesus will come to them in a loving, prayerful way. Loving God by loving lost people is the greatest and

45

Figure 2

Does Your Vision Exceed What You Can See?

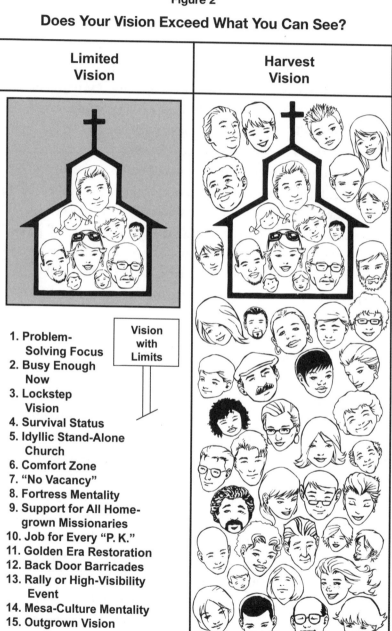

Limited Vision	Harvest Vision

Limited Vision

1. Problem-Solving Focus
2. Busy Enough Now
3. Lockstep Vision
4. Survival Status
5. Idyllic Stand-Alone Church
6. Comfort Zone
7. "No Vacancy"
8. Fortress Mentality
9. Support for All Home-grown Missionaries
10. Job for Every "P. K."
11. Golden Era Restoration
12. Back Door Barricades
13. Rally or High-Visibility Event
14. Mesa-Culture Mentality
15. Outgrown Vision

Vision with Limits

the only limitless motivator I have ever observed. As Bill Hybels often says in describing his vision for what became North America's attendance-leading church, Willow Creek Community Church, "Lost people matter to God. Therefore, lost people should matter to me."

Before you entered the mission field represented by your church, God went first.

How to Listen in Prayer

I cannot speak of vision without also underscoring the role of fasting and prayer. In my consulting, when I ask pastors how they seek God on this issue of vision, most will affirm that they make it their practice to claim such promises as Jesus's words about asking, seeking, and knocking (Matt. 7:7–8). Almost none of these pastors talk about listening to God. The most common approach, I suspect, is to continue talking while waiting on God to answer. I propose that our fervency in speaking seriously undercuts our ability to hear God's reply.

A story Dr. David Yonggi Cho recounted in my hearing summarizes the essence of what prayer could be all about. He said that when Yoido Full Gospel Church had reached about three hundred thousand active participants, a pastor from a church of three thousand came to see him. The pastor said, "Dr. Cho, I need help in understanding something. Like yourself, I'm a Korean and am pastor of a church. But you have three hundred thousand and I have three thousand, so something does not add up for me."

Then this pastor, without any hint of arrogance, began to compare his background with that of Dr. Cho. "I have an American education, you have studied only at a Bible school here in Korea. In addition, I have examined, as objectively as I can, tape recordings of my sermons and of your sermons. I believe I preach a better sermon. What I don't understand is why, if I preach a better sermon and have a better education, do you have three hundred thousand people in church and I have three thousand people."

47

Dr. Cho said that he answered with a question. "Do you pray?"

"Oh, yes," the minister said.

"How much?"

He answered, "I pray daily at least thirty minutes. I've outlined my prayers so that in the course of the week I've prayed for all my obligations here and across the world. I'm very, very conscientious about that."

> Prayer is not so much an effort as a communion.

After pausing, the visiting pastor asked Dr. Cho, "How much do you pray?"

Dr. Cho answered, "Anywhere between one and three hours a day."

Then came the clincher. "The difference," Dr. Cho said, "between thirty minutes and one to three hours is the difference between three thousand and three hundred thousand."

My thoughts raced to my own prayer life. *One to three hours a day?* I asked myself. *What in the world could I say for up to three hours in one day?* After thirty minutes I'm prayed up and am beginning to talk in circles. How does someone pray for hours on end?

Then I realized the Western assumptions through which I was hearing Dr. Cho's story. What kind of social abnormality would I need to hold a "conversation" in which, nonstop for three hours, I did all the talking?

When we first hear Dr. Cho's story, we think, *Okay, take the thirty-minute stuff we do and draw it out five times as much. Try harder and push longer.* Greater energy leads to more vigorous praying, according to the Western mind-set.

Does Dr. Cho talk *to* God all that time, or does he talk *with* God? The fundamental redefinition of prayer we need is this: prayer is not so much an effort as a communion. If I do not give God as much time to talk to me as I spend talking to Him, I am off balance. No wonder, then, that I did not receive vision and guidance from Him.

Prayer Is More Than "Trying Harder"

Westerners may believe God honors hard prayer, but that is not always the case in Scripture. For instance, Elijah's style, like that of Avis car rentals and of most pastors, seemed to be "We Try Harder." In his ordeal with the prophets of Baal, he so exhausted himself that he became suicidally depressed. "Lord," he said (to paraphrase 1 Kings 18 and 19), "I'm done. I'm checking out. Just show me the fight ring so I can throw in the towel. All I want to do is die."

How did God reply? "Elijah, your prayers are not finished yet. Go down to the cave. Rest. Eat something. Stay there until you hear from Me."

That is when Elijah received a better idea. After he poured out all his despair to the Lord, he was finally ready to listen. "Elijah," God said. "The work I'm getting ready for you is much bigger than anything done to date. We need another king and a new helper for you."

Elijah went from that place of listening prayer to anoint Elisha the great prophet and to anoint a new king. These people, in turn, did far more than silence four hundred false prophets on Mount Carmel. They cleaned out Baal worship all across Israel.

SELF-EVALUATION MOMENT

1. In the last week, how much time per day did you average in prayer?

2. Is your initial reaction, in writing down a specific number, one of guilt for not "doing more"? If so, why do you feel that way?

3. If you were to experiment with listening prayer, how would you do it? For example, where would you go? How much time would you need to block out? What distractions would you anticipate, and how would you deal with them?

4. Will you commit yourself, within the next week, to go before the Lord in listening prayer?

I, too, have experienced the powerful, refreshing results of listening prayer. As a pastor, before entering church consulting ministry, I was faced with a situation in my town where racial segregation sharply divided blacks from whites. We organized our college kids and invited hundreds of African American children to our summer Bible school programs. They came, but their parents would not. We knew we would not be able to sustain the parenting role toward these children over the decades that discipleship required, so we began to seek the Lord's guidance as to how to meet this great need.

I recently participated in the fortieth anniversary of this church that had arisen to make disciples among the children. After we had opened our church and schools to all races, it became clear that once the barrier to attending was removed, the black adults preferred to organize their own congregation with their own leadership. Our prayers led us to realize that evangelism among the parents of the children would lead to the most enduring discipleship. We refocused our efforts toward parents, and a black-led church resulted. I participated in the ordination of the son of the pastor as he was called to succeed his retiring minister father. He asked how we had come to sponsor the church. I shared that he and his classmates were the reason we set out after his parents so they would provide the spiritual parenting needed to bring him and his classmates to maturity. He was the answer to our prayers. Our strategy was the result of seeking God's face and listening until we knew what to do. The fruit has endured.

The Bottom Line in Prayer

What am I saying? When you learn to pray in such a way that you listen, you will not only find out what God wants to be done but you will begin to learn the by *whom*, the *how*, and the *when*. As a result, you can proceed with enormous boldness. When you are doing God's work in God's way and in God's time, then you are God's person and you are the most invincible force on earth. All the opposition you can face will be irrelevant.

The crucial issue boils down to one of faith: the ability to see what God is ready to do next so that you are in a cooperative attitude as He does that. That is what it means to walk by faith.

When Elijah stood at Mount Carmel (see 1 Kings 18), he was not bossing God around. He did not say, "Put the fire there, God," as though it was all Elijah's bright idea. The thing that made Elijah a survivor of Mount Carmel was that he knew how far away to stand from that pile of wet wood.

He had heard what God had called him to do, and he did not get in the way. His prayer was, "Lord, I am here, because You told me to come here. That wood over there is wet because You told me to wet it. These people have been gathered together because You told me to gather them together. So, Lord, we are here simply because we have been following orders."

Until we are aware of God's marching orders, our activities are vain and foolish. Bill Hybels wrote a book entitled *Too Busy Not to Pray*. It says, in essence, that a human being's "engine" is designed to run at 5,000 rpm but he was regularly winding his out at 10,000 rpm. He tells of having to slow down, through journaling and other exercises, so that he could hear God.⁴

I have every confidence, then, that the astounding growth of Willow Creek Community Church has come not because Bill Hybels said, "I want the biggest church in North America." Rather, he said, "I want to abide in Jesus Christ," and then he was able to receive the vision God had for the spiritual harvest Willow Creek is to reach. The same could be said of many other churches, small and large, here and around the world.

That is the kind of vision God longs to give to all who will seek Him.

FOR FURTHER THOUGHT

1. Do you agree that the fifteen vision limiters described do indeed put a cap on the scope of ministry that a church might try to achieve? Pick six of the vision limiters that seem clearest to you; which biblical principles would support or challenge each one?

2. Select four of the vision limiters and give examples for each that would be applicable to your church. Which vision limiter has the strongest influence on your church?

3. In what ways is the following quotation from this chapter applicable to your church? "Before you entered the mission field represented by your church, God went first. Before you arrived there, He had already sowed. The prayers of mothers, the gospel preaching of others, and the witness of Christians before you have all been used by God to prepare a harvest."

4. How are the experiences of Bill Hybels and David Yonggi Cho relevant to the church you now serve? In what way do they challenge you? What has been your experience with "listening prayer"?

5. Summarize in twenty-five words or less your vision for the church you presently serve. In what ways is that vision inadequate when compared with the size of harvest God might use your church to reach?

How Does Vision Motivate?

I recently met with a pastor who wanted to take his church to a new level but didn't know how to change himself to lead it there. In recent months his church had seen surges of new life, and each time it was a bit painful for both him and the congregation to adjust to the new realities that growth had brought. As he spoke with me, I could sense he had a powerful vision of the harvest God wanted to bring to that congregation. But where should he start, and what should he do differently?

Likewise, suppose you have a growing conviction of what God is calling your church to be and do. You see where you are now (point A), what improvements and changes need to be introduced (point B), and where you will move for the future (point C). You are eager and excited.

But now what do you do? You know you cannot start at point C. How do you go to work on point B? And how do you shift your own role while leading your congregation through these transitions?

Communication Counts

Such books as *Leaders: Strategies for Taking Charge*, by Warren Bennis and Burt Nanus, describe how visionary leadership operates.

These authors say: "The leader may generate new views of the future and may be a genius at synthesizing and articulating these new views of the future, but this makes a difference only when the vision has been successfully communicated throughout the organization and effectively institutionalized as a guiding principle."[1]

A vision in an organization cannot be established by edict or by the exercise of power or coercion. It is more an act of persuasion, of creating an enthusiastic and dedicated commitment because it is right for the times, right for the organization, and right for the people who are working in it.

Similarly, in Christ's church, God often works through the vision of a leader. David Yonggi Cho, founding pastor of the world's largest church, developed more than fifty thousand trained cell-group leaders among a worship attendance of over half a million. These trained caregivers accepted that role because Dr. Cho had a vision of what would happen if he would release laypeople to care for one another. The tools he put in their hands, the supervision system he inaugurated, and the staff he hired all contributed to the vision being a reality.[2]

> A vision in an organization cannot be established by edict or by the exercise of power or coercion.

Did Jesus convey a picture and pathway to the future? I believe He spread His vision of the kingdom of God through His analogies and stories. Jesus frequently addressed, "What is the kingdom of God like?" His answers were filled with vivid and powerful word pictures: "[It] is like a man who sowed good seed" (Matt. 13:24), or "like a mustard seed" (v. 31), or "like yeast" (v. 33). When a pastor today says, "What is the church like?" or "I have a dream," and then uses an analogy to describe a preferred future, that minister is likewise casting or communicating vision.

Sermon lore contains the story of an elocutionist who visited a church and read aloud Psalm 23. Then an old man, who was a longtime member and had suffered greatly over the years, stood up and prayed. In his conversation with God he quoted that same psalm.

The audience did not applaud him as they did the public speaker. Instead, they wept. Afterward someone said to the elocutionist, "Can you account for the difference in how these people responded to you and how they responded to him?" He replied, "Yes, I knew the psalm *about* the Shepherd, but he *knew* the Shepherd." The veteran follower of Christ knew more than the written Word of God. He had communed with the Creator of the universe and had been shaped by the vision of his best Friend. Closeness to God like that is an essential source of vision for all leaders and leadership teams.

How Is Vision Cast (Communicated)?

Once you have a sense of God's vision, how do you communicate it? Three elements, when combined, help people believe a vision and take ownership in it.

1. First, you need a game plan.

What is your outline for making the most effective use of your pastoral leaders' abilities for the lives of your staff and your laypeople? What is your strategy to best enable laypeople to give greatest support to their pastor's plans for the church?

For some churches the formula is as simple as this: celebrate in festivals and care in cells. Another way to describe that particular game plan would be to say the goal is to multiply the ministry of Jesus by empowering lay leaders to provide pastoral care to groups of about ten people.

The game plan, then, is your philosophy of ministry. It summarizes your overall strategy and objectives. It needs to be clear enough that you could present it in three or four sentences to your unchurched neighbor who asks, "Exactly what is your church trying to do?"

Here are some game plans that convey a focused direction for a church:

"Our purpose is loving God, caring for one another, and reaching the world for Christ."

"God is building an ever-stronger church, with ongoing emphasis on evangelism, discipleship, and nurture, that will reach metro (name of city) and beyond."

"Our vision is to touch our world with the love of Christ as we grow in His Spirit and reach out in love, motivated by a passion for Christ and compassion for others."

"Using every available opportunity in all walks of life to lovingly persuade the world to become committed followers of Jesus Christ and responsible members of His growing kingdom, that they may do the same."

"Our mission is to be a worshiping people, a caring community, a preaching center, an equipping network, and a worldwide witness."[3]

2. A second factor that helps the vision is the party line.

In other words, how are the various truths of the faith handled at your church? Which are perceived as having high priority? Examples of party line are: "We don't do tongues here," "If you want the church to pray for healing, ask the elders to come and anoint you with oil," and "Unless you lead a home-cell group, you cannot get elected to office at this church." The party line, then, may deal with some very ticklish issues. But it is a necessary ingredient in explaining how a vision will be communicated.

3. A third component of effective vision casting is hero making.

Michael LeBoeuf, in his book *The Greatest Management Principle in the World*, says, in essence, "What gets rewarded gets done."[4] The implication for pastors and church leaders is to keep score and then brag on the things they want to see more of.

Christians profit from positive role models, whether they come from the hall of champions in Hebrews 11, from a video profile of an amazing volunteer, or from hero-making sermons. As the old adage goes, "Everybody loves a story." One of the reasons for the renewed interest in narrative preaching is that people love to learn about people. Stories communicate vision as they set a norm for what it means to be a winner.

SELF-EVALUATION MOMENT

Which of the three persuasion methods below best represent your style of vision casting? Which example includes all above-mentioned elements of vision casting?

1. "I want to thank everyone who contributed to the Christmas food drive and to announce that, probably due to everybody being so busy, only Nathan Kenion had the time to deliver the baskets. You need to thank him and make a little extra time next year when we run the food drive. It's important, you know!"

2. "Did everyone hear how Nathan Kenion made sure every food basket was delivered on Christmas Eve? That's the kind of ministry our church wants to be known for! Thanks to Nathan's initiative, we showed twenty new households what it means to know Christ and make him known."

3. "I'm happy to report that our food drive was a great success, and that we made sure every basket was delivered by Christmas Eve. We on the staff really feel supported by you, and your staff is really glad that together we got this special project accomplished."

Only example 2 incorporates all three elements of vision casting in positive terms. Example 1 affirms that the food drive is "very important" to the game plan, appeals to guilt and duty as the party line, and makes a hero of Nathan. Example 3 speaks of the food drive as a special project, urges loyalty to the staff as the party line, and makes heroes of the staff, not of Nathan.

What Helps Prevent Vision Failure?

To be better prepared to launch your vision in your church, you need to consider four ingredients that need to be in place before you can safely assume that the vision is complete. Our field observations of actual leaders and churches confirm that prematurity is the most common cause of vision failure.

First, know that the vision answers the *what* question. In other words, you see what God wants accomplished in this particular place. The immature vision maker will take the *what* information and start running. But knowing what to do is only part of the guidance God intends to give.

Second, know *how* God wants it done. Numerous Old Testament accounts illustrate that God not only told His children what He wanted them to do but He frequently told them how to do it. The procedures for constructing the ark, the tabernacle, and many other elements of God's plan were spelled out in enormous detail. The *how* was very significant.

Third, know *by whom* the vision should be done. God Almighty, Creator and Overseer of the entire universe, frequently thought it important to spell out who should be involved in the process. "Use the tribe of Judah to start the battle against the Benjamites' left-handed slingers" (see Judg. 20:13–18), or "I have filled Bezalel with the Spirit of God and with skill, ability, and knowledge" in the crafts needed for the tabernacle construction (see Exod. 31:1–11; 35:30–36:1). God often fingers the specific talents He wants to use.

This specific guidance is evidenced in Loren Cunningham's work with Youth With A Mission. He tells of speaking to a crowd of several hundred and noticing, in particular, a young man wearing a green sweater. After the meeting, Cunningham's wife, Darlene, told her husband that not only did the same eighteen-year-old catch her attention, but that she heard God tell her to "speak to a boy in a green sweater" about coming on their summer program.

Darlene found the young man and related to him what God had told her minutes before. The youth was dumbfounded. He kept hitting his chest with his open palm. "Uh, I . . . I just asked God to have one of you speak to me personally if He wanted me to go!"

The book containing this account, *Is That Really You, God?*, observes that in the twenty years between the "green sweater" event and the writing of the book, an enormously fruitful ministry came out of that person.[5] God gave Loren and Darlene Cunningham "by whom" guidance. God answers the "by whom" question in numerous ways: Scripture illuminated by the Holy Spirit, godly counsel, impressions on the heart, divinely shaped circumstances, and—as with the Cunninghams—the still, small voice of God. The key is to be aware that "by whom" issues are of great significance. They play an important role in how a vision takes shape.

Fourth, know *when* is the right time to act. I once sat with Christian philosopher Francis Schaeffer. I said, "Dr. Schaeffer, the genius of your ministry draws on your ability to stroke your beard in a hesitating way, and then to offer very simple maxims, timed in such a way and with such an inimitable style that people are leaning forward in eagerness to hear what you will say next. That dynamic is perfect for video and film. You would bestow a wonderful gift on evangelical Christianity if you would allow yourself to be filmed walking along some outdoor trail in Switzerland and commenting on life."

He stroked his beard (of course!) and said, "Hmmm. This is confirming."

After pausing (of course!) he said, "It will take a great deal of discernment and prayer for me to know who the production company should be, what the visual format should look like, and whether it is God's time yet or not."

Two years later, the film series *How Shall We Then Live?* was released. It produced such a widespread impact, I believe, because Dr. Schaeffer had not grabbed a general idea and started running with it. Rather, the vision had matured. He understood all the pieces before he moved.

> The King's business requires haste, but God is not hasty.

Scripture abounds with illustrations of how God sometimes moves very quickly. Those examples do not mean that God is in a hurry, however. The King's business requires haste, but God is not hasty.

What Vision Can Do

In one twelve-month period, the worship attendance at Willow Creek Community Church near Chicago jumped by almost three thousand. The year was 1986, and it grew from an average weekly attendance of 5,606 the previous year to one high-attendance Sunday of 8,248.

At that time, I asked Bill Hybels, the founding pastor, "What does it feel like to experience a 50 percent jump in one year's time?"

He said, "We had no idea how rapidly the growth would occur; it caught us completely by surprise. We fill the auditorium twice, and have to bring in folding chairs as well."

Then he made a comment that revealed the scope of his vision. "We're really struggling," he said, "because no one is willing to bar our doors and say to lost people who drive into our parking lot, 'We haven't made provision for you to hear the gospel today. You'll have to go home now.'"

I asked Pastor Hybels what he was planning to do. He shook his head. "We don't know fully. We've prayed, we've sought, we've searched. We think we're going to try a Saturday night service. We're not sure it will work, but we've got to do something."

I said, "Have you ever wanted to quit growing?"

He answered, "There was a time when I remember us saying, 'Hey, we've grown enough. Let's cool it for a while.'"

He continued, "We decided to change our focus. Instead of trying to make every Sunday more appealing than the week before, I'd launch a ten-week series on the Ten Commandments. That was the most unexciting topic for unsaved people I could think of. I figured it would cap the growth and give us a breather.

"To our surprise, our attendance increased by one thousand during that series! We felt like God reached down and slapped us. Soundly rebuked, I said, 'Lord, we won't ever try to slow you down again!'"

Bill Hybels, who believes his primary spiritual gift is leadership, understands the what, how, by whom, and when components of vision. By the grace of God, his maturity of vision will result in the church continuing to go forward.

Needed: A Balanced Team[6]

I am often asked, "Can *any* godly leader improve his or her vision-implementing skills? Can I develop ways of thinking that will give me a more consistent performance and higher-quality decisions than at present?" I believe the answer is yes.

Surveys show that most pastors and lay leaders excel either as doers or as dreamers, but not as both. That is, some preoccupy themselves with activity and implementation, while others spend lots of time thinking of great things to be done for God but do not know how to transform those dreams into reality. For greatest effectiveness, a leader must know how to provide direction by both dreaming and doing.

A leader must know how to provide direction by both dreaming and doing.

Many pastors and key laypeople have not reached their full, God-given potential in how to lead a team that can make things happen. Certain techniques, skills, and sensitivities can help them move from being do-aholics or idealists to being actual leaders, and so can developing a leadership team where both qualities are represented.

Joel Barker, a bestselling author on the topic of paradigm shifts, says, "A leader is someone you will follow to a place you wouldn't go by yourself."[7] In other words, a leader is someone who has a follower. No functional definition of leadership will hold up in the absence of followers.

To increase one's effectiveness at influencing a "followership," a leader needs to maintain balance on both the "dreaming" and the "doing" portions of providing direction.

But there is more to leadership. According to Max DePree, former board chairman of an evangelical seminary and chief executive officer of a multimillion-dollar business, "In the art of leadership . . . the first responsibility of a leader is to define reality."[8] Leaders cause their followers to know what is important and what is not. Whether in church or business, they describe the landscape, articulate the plan of action, and rally the troops to join in the effort.

How, then, does a leader or leadership team begin to implement God's vision for a particular church?

1. The first step is to clearly articulate the desired outcome.

What do you believe God wants to see happen? Obviously, if you do not know what the improvement is supposed to look like, then you will not know when you have arrived.

In Bill Hybels's case, the desired outcome was that Willow Creek would never have to turn anyone away who comes seeking God. For him and his leadership team, this vision means keeping enough open seats in the auditorium so as not to create a turn-away factor.

2. The second step in implementing vision is to tackle the blockage problem.

What is preventing the outcome from taking place? That question requires some analysis. Sometimes the answer is obvious. Other times the formula is so complicated that you need help, such as from a professional consultant, to identify the blockage.

For example, several years ago, a pastor said to me, "I've been studying our church and I think we're experiencing sociological strangulation."

I asked for his evidence.

"Well," he said, "our attendance has plateaued at 120 and we need a larger auditorium." It turned out, however, that his present auditorium held 200 seats. Strangulation does not occur until a church exceeds 80 percent—160 seats, in this case.[9]

"I don't think tearing down your auditorium and building it larger is really the answer," I said. "Let's talk about your Christian education space. If you started a new Sunday school class tomorrow, where would you place it?"

"In one of the empty rooms down at the end of the hall," he quickly responded. "We're temporarily using them for storage."

"Well," I said, "the Sunday school doesn't seem to be in trouble. So we haven't identified the blockage yet. How about parking?"

"We're in great shape," he answered. "We just paved the alley behind the church and we gained twelve parking spaces."

My surveys have shown that the average car on a Sunday morning contains about 2.3 people. (That's a husband with a wife who is three months pregnant!) So, with an attendance of 120, he would need just over fifty parking spaces.

"What does the rest of your parking look like?" I asked.

"Those twelve new spaces represent our entire on-premises parking," he said.

"Oh! Where do the other forty or so cars park?" I queried.

"They park curbside," he said.

"What distance do they have to walk from curbside?"

"Oh, one or two hills."

I suspected we had found the blockage. "Hills? Do you have much ice here during the winter?"

"Sure, lots, but our people get used to it."

"Do you plow the sidewalks?"

"What sidewalks?"

Now I knew we had found a major problem. "What about a woman wearing heels and carrying a baby?"

"It's an adventure, but our people can handle it!" he acknowledged with a smile.

"Where do you park *your* car?" I asked. I could not understand how this intelligent pastor had missed the significance of the parking issue.

"In my garage," he explained. "It's in the manse next door to the church. One or two other families also live adjacent to the church building, and all we do is walk across the alley."

Here was a pastor who could not see his problem with low parking capacity because he never had to use the lot. Nor did two other families, who happened to be opinion leaders on the church board.

3. The third step in vision implementation is to act.

I suggested to the pastor that the church tear down the manse and make the property into a parking lot. However, in his denomination that was unthinkable, especially since the manse looked like a historical artifact from the frontier era.

Even if my proposal was unacceptable, and the Lord did not send a lightning bolt, the church at least knew what issue to work on. Eventually, as I recall, they bought a nearby empty lot and made it suitable for parking.

This process of moving from outcome statement to blockage identification to action is not intuitive. Most church leaders are talented for one of these steps but not all three.

People who are drawn to outcome issues tend to be visionaries, while people who live near the action box tend to be doers. What about those skilled in detecting blockages? I call them observers or analysts. Such people are rarely pastors.

Depending on how God has wired you, one of these categories will seem most natural for you. Chances are that you seldom venture willingly beyond the comfort of that arena.[10]

SELF-EVALUATION MOMENT

It's fun to guess the motivation of different people in your church. (Or would only an analyzer make a statement like that?) With which of the following people do you most closely identify? Which is most like your spouse, your pastor, or another member of the pastoral team?

Maria: She sits at meetings strumming her fingers or tapping her foot. She loves to make lists, with lots of specifics, down to the exact quantities of postage and coffee needed. "Now that's real planning," she'll say. When the pastor or another leader talks about the grand purposes and ideals envisioned for the church, she says, "Let's get on with it! When are we going to *do* something?" (Maria's drawback: If she alone were directing the planning process, she'd churn out lists of things to do, but they may go nowhere, because her action steps would not necessarily address the blockages that lead to an outcome.) Maria is a doer.

Charlie: He begins many comments with "I noticed that . . ." or "I was thinking about . . ." At the same time, he does not seem motivated to solve the problem; he would much rather talk about it—or find another conundrum to untangle. (Charlie's drawback: If he alone were directing the planning process, he would inspire great discussions and marvelous insight, but little action.) Charlie is an observer.

Pete: He doesn't even like planning meetings. He's forever talking about the purposes of God and what God wants to see done at the church. He becomes so passionate about his dreams for the ministry that people rib him about not being able to eat breakfast in the morning until he's had at least twelve new ideas. (Pete's drawback: If he alone were directing the planning process, he might become very frustrated that the church is more on dead center than exploding with vitality. In addition, he probably wouldn't be able to figure out why the process is not working.) Pete is a visionary.

Making It Work

A Methodist pastor in Philadelphia, known as the most advanced urban-ministries person in his section of the district, once said to me, "Now I finally understand why I've been spinning my wheels for the last five years."

I asked him to explain. He told me about an earlier era at the same church, which was quite successful. "I'm an idea man," he said. "I'd get an inspiration, and then it would turn into ministry."

As we talked, it became clear that he was a visionary. He did not know *how* his ideas had translated into ministry, because a layman in his church had taken care of that.

"This guy spent his entire life organizing labor unions," the minister explained. "When he retired, he got converted, joined our church, and hung around my elbow. I'd give someone a wonderful ministry idea and, as I turned to talk with somebody else, he'd go off to the side with whomever I'd just talked to and suggest ways to implement my suggestions. Before I knew it, they had a whole ministry planned.

"He'd come back, listen to me talking to the next person, follow that person, and give that individual some guidelines as well.

"Ever since this man died," continued the minister, "I haven't made a lick of progress."

His summary statement was telling. "Until just now I didn't realize what that guy did for our church. I visualized and he organized."

This Methodist minister had found someone whose forte was the observer's box, who analyzed, helped the doers get their task lists together, and translated vision into an "actionable" game plan.

In whichever area you excel, do you see what you can do? If you are going to move beyond yourself, link up with people whose strengths differ from yours. Doing so could give birth to a complete problem-solving team.

FOR FURTHER THOUGHT

1. Recall from Scripture some of Jesus's commands that communicate a strong sense of vision. What are some experiences in the book of Acts in which the church struggled with the issue

of vision? What specific vision did God give the apostle Paul for his ministry? Peter?

2. Think of a recent goal that your church met with great success. Review how well the what, how, by whom, and when components were articulated. What correlation do you see between successful implementation and maturity of vision? What would be an example of a premature vision in your fellowship?

3. Among your pastoral leadership and church board, who are the visionaries? The analyzers? The doers? If you have had a recent change of pastoral leadership, what were the strengths of the previous minister? What expectations were then transferred to the successor?

4. Think about the last time you tried to "sell" a new idea to someone in your church. Did you include elements of the game plan? Of party line? Of hero making?

How Would an Outsider Describe Your Church?

It is common knowledge that people with diabetes can live healthy, productive lives if they can receive regular injections of insulin.

When the human body breaks down food, sugars enter the blood and the pancreas produces insulin to regulate the blood's glucose level. If that fails, the result is diabetes, a condition that causes dangerous health effects: weight loss, increasing weakness and melancholy, failure of vital organs, and finally coma and death.

Because scientific researchers have discovered the essential role the pancreas's production of insulin plays in human health, they have developed a way to inject specific quantities of it into the bloodstream of a diabetic person so that the metabolizing of sugars occurs as if the pancreas were functioning normally.

Systems Thinking as a Helpful Tool

What these researchers have done is called *systems thinking*. They asked: What does the body do with sugar? What hormone is necessary to regulate carbohydrate metabolism, to control the blood sugar? As they traced the effects of sugar through the human system and found what was not functioning well, they could compensate for it.

Why, humanly speaking, has your church grown, or not grown?

Systems thinking, then, leads to accurate diagnosis and intelligent compensation.

Systems thinking, likewise, is needed in a church each time someone asks questions such as: Why are we growing, or not growing? Where are leaders being developed, or not developed? What needs to be fixed? If the "pancreas" is not operative, do we need a substitute for it?

An important step, then, in analyzing whatever growth barrier your church faces is to examine what has worked in the past and what has not. In short: Why, humanly speaking, has your church grown, or not grown?

SELF-EVALUATION MOMENT

Before reading further, apply a systems perspective to your church.

1. What are the top two factors God has used to produce growth in your church over recent years?
2. What, at present, is not functioning well?
3. How does that insulin equivalent need to be replaced or compensated for?

Bayer, Bufferin, or Generic?

Let me carry the idea of a systems perspective one step further by using the analogy of aspirin research.

I liken the state of the church today to the pharmaceutical industry of the late nineteenth century. Back then, German laboratories were learning to identify and synthesize compounds. One of their developments is what we today call aspirin.

The substance, consumed by the American public at the rate of twenty tons a year, is a derivative of an acid found in the bark of a willow tree. For centuries people had found relief from their tooth-aches, headaches, joint pains, and the like by chewing on willow bark. In time, various manufacturers sold extracts of willow bark.

As the study of pharmacology developed, researchers analyzed the family of willow trees to find the active ingredients that relieved people's pain. Was the yellow color necessary? No, that came from the tar on the bark. How about the crunchiness? No, that was the fiber that gives the bark its firmness. What about the bitter taste? Yes, that stemmed from the compound itself, acetylsalicylic acid.

In 1893 Felix Hoffman, of the Bayer Company of Germany, de-veloped a commercial process for the production of acetylsalicylic acid. He and his colleagues could do so because they had come to understand the molecular structure, and thus the active ingredients, of what was to become the world's most widely used medication.

The net result is that when you swallow or chew an aspirin tablet, you can be confident that all the vital ingredients have been included. You know that your Bayer, Bufferin, Anacin, or generic-brand aspirin will contribute to your feeling better.

The same story could be told of the sociology of church orga-nizations. All our various denominations have been chewing willow bark or taking willow extract. As we study the different things that work, however, we begin to distinguish between the necessary active ingredients and the nice-to-have peripheral stuff like orange color or cherry flavor.

Similarly, by clearly identifying the underlying compounds at work in churches, we can relieve a lot more pain without the distractions of tree tar, sap, dust, bugs, and everything else that may accompany our bark.

Conversely, if we try to build a church on methodology alone, we will wind up chewing on a panacea that offers no long-term relief to our pain, fever, or inflammation.

Not What You May Think

Many pastors and lay leaders, in answering the question of why their church has grown or not grown, experience an eye-opening revelation. My discoveries on this topic trace back to my young adult years.

After being reared in Miami and educated elsewhere in the South, I became a pastor in Gainesville, Florida. As a result, I thought I was a Southerner. At the Gainesville church, however, one of our visitors, a big, pompous surgeon, walked up to me, stamped his foot, and said, "This is a Northern church. I like it, and I'll be back."

My first thought was, *How could he sum us up like that? What makes us Northern? How could he so misdiagnose us?*

I thought I already knew the difference between the two. In many Southern churches they compliment the preacher's histrionics, sweat, and use of guilt motivation to trample on people's toes. I thought I qualified.

Then a highway patrolman visited the church. When I returned the call, he said, "Your church is as real as my thumb, preacher, but I won't be back."

"Why not?" I asked.

"Because you're not a Southern church," he said.

I was hearing two witnesses, one intellectually arrogant and another a common country fellow, and they both said the same thing.

Some years later, a teacher who became my mentor, C. Peter Wagner, helped me make sense of what had transpired. My dad was from Gallipolis, Ohio, and my mother was from Kearney, Nebraska. Those Midwestern German and English backgrounds influenced me more than all the palm trees of Miami. The genetics and culture I carried, even the way I perceived humor, was something as Midwestern as if I were a pastor in Peoria, Illinois.

With guidance from Dr. Wagner and others, I reflected on that pastorate and realized the people drawn to our church were largely from Iowa, Michigan, Illinois, Ohio, Pennsylvania, and New York.

Why did these Northerners come under my leadership? I used to think it was my God-given charisma. As it turns out, I had not captivated them; I was merely the least bad of their options.

When they came to our town, they scouted around for a Baptist church. Gainesville boasted twelve Baptist churches of the Southern variety, but only our church represented the Northern variety. No one had noticed that the reason our church was growing was because Midwesterners were migrating to our area.

I thought I was there by the call of God, and I was. But He knew more about cultural match than I did, and that is probably why I was brought to that place. I think the Lord looked at what He had going down there and said, "I'm missing a Midwestern unit in that region. If I bring that fellow named George over to Gainesville, it will all work." The church was a wonderful success, but because of factors that were beyond my awareness.

If you had asked me why the church went from zero to 650 in nine years, I, like most pastors, would have offered this ready reply: "We preach the Bible." At that point in my own development I was not trained in social research, so it never occurred to me to test that proposition. What if I had investigated all the other churches in that region to find out how many others were teaching the Bible as God's authoritative Word? Had I done so, I would have discovered many churches with that same conviction yet little growth to show for it.

Genuine Conversion Growth?

I also made another humbling discovery. I had thought God was using my preaching to lead most of our newcomers to faith in Christ.

It turns out that six of ten people who came into our church had already converted somewhere else. And of the four who "walked the aisle" (the tradition in our church), most had already made their decision to accept Christ before they came to that service.

The picture became more clear when I began consulting. I remember walking into an old Lutheran church and being introduced as Pastor George. My speech does not betray an accent, and, based on a name like George, I do not seem to have German roots, as many Lutherans do.

I sensed that the people were having trouble accepting me. Then, when I mentioned that my wife is an Erhard, their suspicions noticeably lessened.

"Oh, an Erhard, how nice," they responded. "This is the man who married the German girl."

I was in! My reception had nothing to do with my intellectual credentials, my doctrine, or my ability as a leader. The critical event occurred when I married into the "right" family.

I saw this happen in other communions as well, like the time I met a fellow named Jones who was ministering in the Covenant Church. I said, "That's strange. I've never met a Jones who rose to national prominence in a Swedish denomination." He said, "If you knew my wife's maiden name, you'd understand."

What is this? The gospel is for "whosoever will," but you cannot cut it in many circles if you fail to marry the right person, if your name is not pronounced a certain way, or if your ancestors do not go back to the "right" country.

Why? Humans are complex beings with accompanying roots, preferences, heritage, and language, all of which convey their values. Like it or not, each human is a culture-carrying being. We each have a spirit, of course. But the more significant factor in our ability to attract and recruit people to a church often has to do with the fact that our roots give us an inside track to people with similar roots.

This view sounds somewhat deterministic. But the determinism apparently existed whether I was aware of it or not. I had to accept a powerful reality: people did not like me because of my sweetness but they responded to my words because of certain commonalities of culture. My background enabled me to communicate with their dreams and hopes and to hold out to them a vision of a better future in which God is redemptive and Jesus is real.

Why Your Church Has Grown

Donald McGavran, founder of America's church growth movement, tells of interviewing one pastor of a growing church who gave the following as the principal reason for its growth: "We preach the Bible as the Word of God and are faithful to it." Then McGavran asked the pastor of the church across the street why he thought his church had *not* grown for the last ten years. His answer, word-for-word, was the same: "We preach the Bible as the Word of God and are faithful to it."[1]

Peter Wagner agrees: "It may not be obvious at first, but it is a fact that many pastors of growing churches have only vague insights into the reasons why their churches are growing."[2] My book *Prepare Your Church for the Future* identifies sixteen different growth sources that most church leaders have either observed or experienced. Here is a summary of those growth sources, which in themselves may be effective methodologies (see also Figure 3).

1. *Preaching and Revivals.* Your church revolves around enthusiastic, firebrand preaching or has experienced genuine revival from an outpouring of the Holy Spirit.
2. *Sunday School.* Your church's growth is fueled by momentum from Sunday school (or whatever name you use for it).
3. *Bus Ministry.* Your church reaches new families through bus captains who knock on doors and shuttle children to special programming.
4. *Feeder and Receptor Patterns.* Your church recycles Christians from other churches.

5. *Intentional Positioning.* Your church targets a specific population segment, such as being the gathering point for marriageable young adults or people in addiction recovery.

6. *Music Center.* Your church attracts musicians and other art lovers through a continual cycle of performances, choirs, and bands.

7. *Pulpit Teaching and Oratory Skills.* Your church is known as a teaching center where people's notebooks may be bigger than their Bibles.

8. *Miracle Ministry.* Your church focuses on signs and wonders such as healing and deliverance.

9. *Capture-by-Committee Involvement.* Your church builds loyalty by putting newcomers on a committee as soon as possible.

10. *Day Schools.* Your church sponsors a Christian school, which serves as a bridge for people to participate in other church activities.

11. *Next-Door-to-the-Right-Institution Syndrome.* Your church draws from a nearby denominational college, hospital, military base, or other institution.

12. *High-Visibility and High-Profile Guests.* Your church features a steady stream of media personalities.

13. *Appealing, Mixed-Media Seeker Services.* Your church combines relevant teaching, artistic expressions, and multimedia entertainment targeted at unchurched young adults who admire innovation.

14. *Multiple Outreach Staff.* Your church staff is comprised of gifted evangelists who pour the bulk of their energies into visitation and outreach.

15. *Immigration and Colonization.* Your church is a large ethnic community, such as Scandinavians or Koreans.

16. *Subcongregations of Adults.* Your church is a collection of large Sunday school classes, women's ministries, or other sizable groups.[3]

Figure 3

Sixteen Growth Methods in Recent History

1. Preaching
and Revivals

2. Sunday
School

3. Bus
Ministry

4. Feeder and
Receptor Patterns

5. Intentional
Positioning

6. Music
Center

7. Pulpit
and Oratory

8. Miracle
Ministry

9. Capture by
Committee

10. Day
Schools

11. Next Door to
Right Institution

12. High-Visibility
Guests

13. Mixed-Media
Seeker Services

14. Multiple
Staff

15. Immigration
and Colonization

16. Subcongrega-
tions of Adults

What an abundance of variables that can combine into a growth pattern! Little wonder that we church leaders have such a hard time making sure our "pancreas" is working—or injecting something to fill in for the insulin that our pancreas fails to produce.

Pacesetters for Every Decade

Pastors and lay leaders continually scan the world for methodologies they find to be impressive and encouraging. In every decade, a different set of high-visibility growing churches have influenced North America's perception or the "insulin injection" needed for greatest church health.

In the 1940s, people trekked to Dallas, Texas, to observe the ministry of W. A. Criswell at First Baptist Church. Or they went to Chattanooga, Tennessee, to see Lee Roberson's great fellowship, Highland Park Baptist Church, with its thirty or more preaching centers.

If you came along a decade later you would have found a different set of churches occupying that special niche of "most imitated." Bus-ministry Sunday school centers were coming of age, so in both the 1950s and 1960s you would have traveled to one of several places that had burst into superchurch and megachurch size, such as Jack Hyles's First Baptist Church of Hammond, Indiana; Dallas Billington's Akron Baptist Temple in Ohio; or Jerry Falwell's Thomas Road Baptist Church in Lynchburg, Virginia.

By the mid-1960s and into the 1970s, new influence centers included the folk mass, the Jesus-people churches, the new charismatic phenomenon, and the larger-than-life intimacy of the body-life movement. One example of this is the church we know today as Calvary Chapel of Santa Ana, California. Founded by Chuck Smith, it built such astonishing youth and music programs that anyone who could make the journey came to listen and learn.

In the 1970s, some of the new pacesetters were the major churches forced out of denominations, such as Central Church of Memphis,

Tennessee, or First Baptist Church of Modesto, California. This generation witnessed the turmoil of Woodstock and a painful era of deindustrialization. Some growth was from islands of conservation in strict teaching churches and other growth was from rising artists and bands in contemporary worship. In retrospect, this decade witnessed unprecedented spiritual conflict, with many reports of demonization and deliverance, as well as the growth of the charismatic movement.

During the 1980s, the rising stars tended to be media centers. The Crystal Cathedral, led by Robert Schuller, rose to prominence in the late 1970s and through its television broadcast gained widespread attention during the 1980s. In one year a quarter of a million people visited to understand its approach to reaching the unchurched.

The 1990s gave rise to a new series of highly influential churches. Willow Creek Community Church, based in the greater Chicago area and led by founding pastor Bill Hybels, broke new ground in its use of seeker-sensitive services, team ministry, and drama and other multimedia. During this decade, T. D. Jakes founded the Potter's House; Guillermo Maldonado started Miami's El Rey Jesus; Perry Noble started NewSpring in Anderson, South Carolina; Andy Stanley launched greater Atlanta's North Point; and Craig Groeschel became pastor of what is known today as Life.Church.

The first decade of the 2000s saw a wave of churches become multisite (one church in two or more locations) and/or multiethnic. Prominent examples include Christ Fellowship of Palm Beach Gardens, Florida; Central Christian Church of greater Las Vegas, Nevada; Lives Changed by Christ of greater Lancaster, Pennsylvania; Elevation Church of greater Charlotte, North Carolina; and Cornerstone Church of San Diego, California—all of which currently have at least five campuses.

Mistaking the Clothing for the Life Underneath

Each of these stellar churches, in introducing its ministry, has tried to articulate why it does what it does. In general, the more plausible and persuasive its explanations, the larger a magnet it becomes, and the more publicity it receives.

Two potential pitfalls accompany this process, however. First, pilgrims to these various thriving churches sometimes take the attitude back home, even if unintentionally, that "If you haven't visited such and such a church and aren't using their approach, you're not with it."

If you go to Second Baptist of Houston, for example, you will undoubtedly be inspired with its passion to reach the lost, even if the manifestation of that zeal is for the male staff, stripped to the waist, to enter a wrestling ring for one of their excitement-building contests. This is a high-energy, aggressive, vibrant church.

At one point the church had bragging rights to owning the largest church facility in Texas. Its primary campus, with a financial value exceeding $100 million, covers acres of buildings. It is both elegant and massive; it fits the "oil sheik" aura of Houston.

While that architectural approach may work in Texas, it is probably inappropriate for Manhattan or downtown Los Angeles. And while entertainment evangelism and attendance contests clearly succeed in many communities, they are not necessarily an imitable philosophy of ministry for a church, say, that is called to reach the academic community of an Ivy League university.

Second, and more importantly, when pastors and lay leaders visit these influence centers, they inevitably go home willing to be innovative and motivated to make changes. But they sometimes try to change their church's clothing rather than the living organism underneath. They have gone to a conference and perceived a method rather than the underlying vital ingredients.

Why does this happen? Maybe the high-visibility church misarticulates why it is growing. Maybe the observer misunderstands the presentation. Or maybe both.

The paradigms in this book are by and large transparent to specific methodologies or worship styles. I believe churches grow

The more important issue is the multiplication of ministry through groups and teams.

best if they find a model that God is blessing. Apparently, then, God is working through a number of different models, from mainstream to pushing-the-edge and the many nuances in between.

But there is more to growth than ministry methodology. The more important issue, no matter what the outward approach looks like, is the multiplication of ministry through groups and teams.

Does a church, and especially its pastor, embody a strong vision for an enlarged harvest? Is a strong desire for growth present? Does the leadership know how to best allocate its time and energy through leadership development and groups? These kinds of issues are the real keys to a more vital future.

The Rationale behind This Chapter

If a team of church growth consultants tried to describe your church, what themes would they highlight? No doubt they would examine growth sources and methodologies being used.

But they would also look underneath and ask if a systemic understanding were informing your perspective. They would probe to make sure you understood how the "insulin" of ministry was being supplied. They would want to make sure that you have distinguished between the cherry flavoring of your aspirin and the molecular compound underneath. In so doing they would point to such issues as vision and coaching.

The purpose of this chapter is to introduce you to the notion of systems thinking beyond methods so that you can make a more accurate diagnosis of your church and therefore more intelligently build on what is essential and compensate for what may be missing.

My point is not to identify a methodology and then leave you there. It is, rather, to help you understand that growth involves more than methodologies, to warn you that many churches misinterpret their growth sources, and to affirm that the most important issue is the vital ingredients of the aspirin, not the color, size, or brand of the particular aspirin tablet.

Armed with this perspective, you are more ready than ever to break barriers to growth.

FOR FURTHER THOUGHT

1. Look over the list of sixteen growth methodologies in this chapter. Which three have most contributed to the growth of your church?
2. What are some of the misconceptions circulating around your church as to why it has grown or not grown?
3. Based on the "vital ingredients" analogy of aspirin research, what do you think are the core factors for the spiritual health and ministry enlargement of any church? Select your top three choices and explain why they are important or will work.
4. What are some of the high-visibility churches that have most influenced you? How would you distinguish between their methodology and their underlying active ingredients?
5. Is there a biblical basis for the idea of one church influencing or mentoring another, or for the concept of more "senior" pastors mentoring newcomer pastors? If the answer is yes, could that training encompass spiritual formation? Managerial skills? Organizational insights?

How Strong Is Your Growth Bias?

What is the reason people come to church? To find God? To find purpose in life? To worship? To be with people they care about? Hopefully all of these motivations are present, but if many pastors are brutally honest, they'll add another reason: by showing up, people help their pastor not feel like a failure.

Many pastors and lay leaders gain a sense of personal value from how they perform at church. Their sense of security, and their evaluation of their church's overall spiritual health, is heavily influenced by whether they are well liked, needed, appreciated, and affirmed.

Leaders and Performers

My prayer in writing this book is that the Spirit of God will grant readers new insight into the nature of ministry. That Bible-based perspective will lead you from being a provider of care *to* your people to being an arranger of care *for* your people. In the process, the spotlight of ministry will shift from your own role and activities to those who provide care to others.

This change is difficult and uncomfortable for most leaders, because they are forever being asked to stand in front of a group. For preachers the temptations of the limelight are even stronger, because their parishioners invariably comment on their performance.

Although being an entertainer is quite different from being a mobilizer, effective leaders do know how to entertain. They understand how to vary their rate, rhythm, volume, and emotional intensity to keep listeners alert. They have mastered the art of holding the attention of an audience.

But performance abilities alone usually cannot grow a church very far. You may keep the audience in stitches, but if you have set no goals toward which the troops are being mobilized, and no organizational channel has been created for dividing the labor, the church will have a hard time going anywhere.

SELF-EVALUATION MOMENT

Think of a recent time that you spoke publicly at church. Which of the following statements represent how you felt afterward?

1. I hope I hear a compliment so I'll know whether or not they liked it.
2. I feel like I gave them a good handle on how to trust God in such and such an area.
3. I bet they noticed that I went a few minutes longer than usual.
4. I made such a hero of Katie Kutcel that I bet the crisis-counseling clinic will be flooded with volunteers.

Based on your answers, how does the concept of entertainment influence your speaking? How does it motivate to mobilize?

Must Your Church Grow to Please God?

Am I saying that every reader of this book has been called by God to lead more people than he or she is ministering to at present?

No. I have no right to make that kind of statement to anyone. Nothing in this book implies that you must build a larger church or spin off daughter or granddaughter churches if you wish to be fully pleasing to our Lord.

My intent, then, is not to induce false guilt. Nor do I suggest any shortcuts to know God and wait on His leading. The only "must" I offer is the need to obey God.

I am certain, however, that God's will for His kingdom involves numerical growth. Many of you, through your prayer life and sensitivity to the Holy Spirit, have the suspicion that God wants to use you as part of that larger work. As such, you are looking for the tools and perspectives necessary to accomplish this larger agenda. It is to such a growth bias that this chapter speaks.

> Nothing in this book implies that you must build a larger church or spin off daughter or granddaughter churches if you wish to be fully pleasing to our Lord.

For many years an organization I led sponsored a seminar named "How to Break the 200 Barrier." Over time it drew almost ten thousand church leaders. After all, the 200-person church faces a growth hurdle that stymies four out of five North American churches.[1]

From the research conducted both during and after these conferences, we have discovered a number of significant facts. First, most seminar attendees had a desire before they came to the event to break a barrier (whether it was 50, 100, 200, or 250). Afterward, 93 percent either agreed or strongly agreed that they left the conference more inspired and encouraged to break their particular growth ceiling and in better possession of the technical knowledge necessary to do so.

The experience at the seminar, then, both strengthened their resolve and caused them to say, "I have the technical knowledge I need." When asked which elements of technical know-how were most fruitful, the alumni invariably gave high ranking to the principle of "sole caregiver to coach and developer of other ministers," described in chapter 1 as moving from being a single caregiver to becoming a maker of caregivers.

Church growth is more a matter of heart first and then of having a certain level of technique.

Second, two-thirds of these alumni reported actual increases in their churches' growth that were larger than could be attributed to seasonal fluctuation. This number is probably low, because the survey included some people who had not been away from the seminar long enough to be able to put their ideas into practice. The actual figure may be 75 percent of alumni who saw increases.

My point is this: numerical church growth can happen, but not simply because of technique. A growth bias stems more from vision than from ministry style. Church growth is more a matter of heart first and then of having a certain level of technique.

It May Feel Funny

Part of the leadership shift involves what the business community calls the move from being a worker to being a manager. That is, the worker personally makes something happen, while the manager's responsibility is to see to it that the job gets done, whether or not the manager has a hands-on role.

This conceptual leap can be difficult, because it may not feel right. I introduced this chapter by referring to how the leader's sense of worth is sometimes tied up in the strokes he or she receives while actually doing primary-care ministry: the bedside, the counseling, even the sermon. Some things, like the sermon, usually cannot be delegated, nor can a number of certain hospital calls, such as those to powerful or longtime members who more or less demand that the senior pastor visit them.

Many leaders will feel awkward trying to conceptualize this new paradigm of day-to-day ministry: that people need care but the clergy are not the only persons who ought to provide this care and, in fact, perhaps should not invest as much time in offering solo primary care as they do in leadership development of other caregivers.

In addition, sometimes parishioners feel uncomfortable with the shift. They expect their clergy to be available. They may even try to pressure the pastor back into the sheepherder mold.

When Chuck Swindoll was senior minister of First Evangelical Free Church of Fullerton, California, a church of more than six thousand people, he described to me the personal pain he experienced during such a transition.

On one occasion, a long-term Sunday school leader came to Dr. Swindoll and said, "Pastor, the last two years, when I invited you to our Sunday school Christmas party, you turned me down. This year I'm not going to take no for an answer. You have to come."

Pastor Swindoll said that the encounter hit a painful nerve. Everything inside him wanted to say yes to this friend.

Instead, he made himself reply, "I turned you down the last two years for the same reason I'm going to turn you down today, and any future year you ask. We now have twenty adult Bible fellowships, all of which have Christmas parties, and if I attend those parties, the Swindoll family will not have Christmas. There would be too much going on. So I've had to decline all invitations."

I could feel Pastor Swindoll's pain as he told how the Sunday school leader walked away in an angry huff. Pastor Swindoll knew that overextending himself further would cause more long-term harm than good—not just through physical fatigue but through keeping him from more direct leadership development. Yet saying no still hurt. He told me that it somehow felt terribly wrong to say no to a member who expected the senior pastor to be available.

Was the Sunday school class really less cared for because the senior pastor did not attend? No. For serious needs, the church had numerous recovery groups and counselors, both lay and professional, on referral for every kind of purpose imaginable.

What about the class's social and fellowship needs? The very gentleman who demanded Pastor Swindoll's attendance was doing an excellent job of providing care for that fifty-or-so-person meeting and was organizing parties all year long. He merely wanted a special treat for his class. He thought that by doing some foot stamping and showing a little edge of belligerency, perhaps he could win for his group what the others had not been able to achieve: the special attention of the senior pastor.

The fact is that no one suffered because of the pastor's absence at the party. The only distress present was inside the member who expected that his senior pastor would, in fact, do all the personal ministry himself, and inside the pastor who wished he could but found himself unable to do so.

Here is a fact many pastors must face: the more inclined the pastor is toward direct personal involvement, the greater his or her struggle in learning to see to it that ministry is done as opposed to doing the ministry alone.

Only by vision marked by a develop-more-caregivers bias can such a hurdle be overcome.

The Inner Turmoil

What is the next development that shapes the vision of someone who wants to lead a flock through the dependency-on-the-clergy barrier and its accompanying limited size?

The vision components are similar in every barrier situation, whether the threshold is 200, 2,000, or 20,000. The leader will recognize where the church is, how it came to be there, and what it needs to do to reach a goal beyond.

This perspective translates itself into an ever-present concern that human beings are desperately in need of having the love of God mediated to them in personal terms. An accompanying passion says that the community of the redeemed, left at its present size, will fall far short of what Jesus Christ would like to accomplish through them.

As that pairing of images permeates the soul of the visionary pastor, the images flesh themselves out through such statements as, "I must commission others to see to it that this work is done, even though certain dear saints, without realizing it, want to limit the growth of the kingdom by restricting care to the personal strength and resources that I as a minister can bring to bear."

What propels a church leader to keep moving forward like that? What can create a "champion" church that accepts and encourages new paradigms of ministry? I believe the answer involves a joining together of both vision and skill.

My son Bob was a javelin thrower in high school. When he first started, his talent was such that his coach encouraged us to get professional training for him. Bob's personal coach, an Olympic medal winner, trained Bob by working out with him. He would say, "You made good progress today. From what I saw, you can get a few more yards if you concentrate on what we did today." I noticed a pattern in his closing conversations—affirmation and encouragement with a reasonable increase in expectation. Bob's skills moved him steadily ahead in competition.

With Bob, as with church leaders, there was a combination of technical proficiencies and an issue of heart. His special trainer knew how one fuels the other, and the net result was that barriers were broken.

Furthermore, in most fields of high accomplishment, mentors, trainers, and models are part of the picture. Champion salespeople seek out other winning salespeople. Champion students seek out other master scholars. People put themselves alongside each other and stretch each other.

Through my years of consulting, I have learned that the pastors who are going to make it in church growth are ones no one has to chase to teach about church growth. They select themselves for breaking barriers, because they dare to dream and imagine that there is a better future out there than the one they have experienced.

The Most Important Growth Bias

I submit that the most important issue in empowerment is a holy imagination of what God can lead a person to become. I believe that in the formation of this sanctified self-image, a Christian can perceive him- or herself as a person who will benefit others by association with them.

This view is not some exaggerated notion of a prideful self. Rather, it stems from the notion that my adequacy comes from a relationship of walking with Christ, and that what I offer to others is provided by an overflow of what I have received from the person of Christ Himself. Jesus said (to paraphrase John 15:4–8), "If you hope to do My will you will have to abide in Me. If you will abide in Me, you will bear fruit in your life."

The privilege of being a person who becomes a positive benefit to others is not based on a magnificent character nor on sinless perfection or high intelligence. Rather, this sense of adequacy springs from staying connected to the person of Jesus Christ. All I need do is let His Word abide in me and consciously depend on His sufficiency.

The most important issue in empowerment is a holy imagination of what God can lead a person to become.

I can speak from experience on what it means to run dry. During one period of my life a pressing schedule and frustrating realization of the yet-unreached harvest led me to a point of such dryness that I felt like an overheated engine that had run out of oil. I found myself so frustrated, dismayed, and angry, so dry and despairing, that one dear friend stopped me and said, "Carl, it is a sin to despair."

He was right. I had looked at the needs so apparent all around me and had thought I was responsible for meeting them all.

Ultimately I confessed, "God, *I* know that I am not adequate, and *You* know that I am not adequate. Now that we've got the facts straight, how about giving me some of Your adequacy here for the task ahead?"

Yet I still held on, thinking I needed to do something to make the difference. I kept using my own strength. I remember driving to a seminar I was to lead. On my way, I held an exhausting phone conversation. A colleague in another state was wrestling with issues so charged that the emotions leaped across the airwaves. I could feel the energy drain out of me.

I could have said, "I have to give a speech in a few minutes and need some time to refresh myself." But I hung up the phone, noticed that the last bit of energy had left my soul, walked into the conference room completely empty, and started speaking anyway.

The next hour and a half was one of the worst of my life. The haunting failure that occurred when I tried to offer inspiration to a group of people, when I had no emotional or spiritual cushion, is a painful memory I will never forget.

In fact, I hope to remember it for this simple reason: the experience was entirely preventable. Had I taken just a few minutes and sung together with the group, prayed with them, spent time in quiet before the Lord, admitted my emptiness, and confessed my need of the Lord's presence, that consulting session would have been redeemed. And the fruit of it would still be apparent today.

What a contrast between that event and the empowerment that could have come from on high! Where was the holy imagination that affirms that a believer can be a channel of the grace of God? That the Christian's very presence gives something that cannot be had otherwise? That the redeemed person is valued not because of a sweet personality, and not because of a great smile, but because in his or her presence Jesus has the freedom to be present too?

The God we serve is the kind who takes unlikely people and makes something beautiful of them. God tells the readers and writers of this book, "You can do it!" In the kingdom of God, unlikely people turn out to be astonishing performers.

Had someone analyzed the apostles Peter or Paul just after their conversions, the conclusion might have been, "You'll probably not become anything significant." Yet God used these two unusual people to turn the whole Roman Empire upside down—or right side up!

If you are a growing Christian, stationed where He wants you to serve, you probably have the capacity to project a growth bias to your people. God can use your encouragement to affirm to your people that He wants to do something special through them.

What would happen if, in the next meeting you lead, you purpose not to use one word of scolding, or even of busying the church with the status quo? What if, instead, you say, "I'm looking at a group of champions. I'm talking to people who can be developed into a victorious army for God."

In the kingdom of God, unlikely people turn out to be astonishing performers.

Or, if you do pulpit ministry, why not spend some of your preparation time imagining how your message will empower your laity for significant ministry? Preach not to the rebellious but to those who have said yes to God and want to go forward.

Have you ever noticed that some sports coaches, no matter where they move around the country, and no matter what the previous records of the ball clubs they currently lead, can produce championship teams?

True, these coaches do tend to attract good players. But there is more. They possess a quality that brings a winning vision to what they are doing.

Your pulpit could be like the locker room at halftime in the big game. What the coach says is not the whole story, because the outcomes are to be found with what the players do when they go back on the field.

The nature of oratorical preaching puts a spotlight on you. In response, you need to swing that spotlight around. You sometimes do that when you say, "Look folks, you are the real stars. The quality of my sermons is not nearly as important as how well your children are turning out. Don't tell me how many times you've been here at the service; instead, talk to me about how you cut off the television or computer and spent time with your spouse praying for the salvation of your neighbors." What you can do beyond exhortation is to build lay ministry vision by describing instances in which caring was done by members and cell-group leaders, sometimes with your assistance and sometimes all by themselves. "This week, Mrs. Atkins told me she was planning a visit to a sick neighbor. She had selected a psalm to read with her and planned to pray with her. I was invited to review the psalm but couldn't have found one more appropriate than the one she used."

Coaching is attitudinal. It contains technical elements, but you will get the technique if you stay with it.

Leading a church is similar. When I was an intern in the ministry, just after graduate school, my pastor had a favorite saying as he went to work with people. He would say, "You know, you're a part of this formula. Whether or not you think you can, you're right!"

The same applies to the climate of your church. Do you have a growth bias? Do you truly believe God will enlarge the scope of your church's harvest? Whether or not you think you can, you're right.

FOR FURTHER THOUGHT

1. Do you agree with the opening comments about performance, entertainment, and mobilizing? Why or why not? What Scripture verses either challenge or affirm each of these motives?

2. Look again at the section "Must Your Church Grow to Please God?" Do you think God calls all churches to numerical growth? What other kinds of spiritual maturation could take place in

a church without being accompanied by eventual numerical growth?

3. How did you feel about how Chuck Swindoll responded to the Sunday school member? Would you have handled it any differently? Have you ever participated in or observed a similar experience?

4. Review the section about abiding in Christ and depending on His sufficiency. What makes the difference between someone who is arrogant and someone who exudes the grace of God?

5. If you are a preacher, do you believe there is any connection between your reward in heaven and your homiletic ability? Would you be pressing the issue too far if you said that God's greatest interest in your message is whether you present your sermon in such a way that your people are moved to obey God?

PART 2

REDEFINE
YOUR ROLE

Why Develop the Skills of a Caregiving Coach?

In a church in which I was pastor, one of our members was a butcher, a massive, muscled man who had once been a professional football player. He was diagnosed with leukemia and, in the course of three weeks, died.

My job, as the "professional," was to break the news to his two little boys. The experience tore me apart. I sat there looking at the boys and realized that absolutely nothing I could say, even though I was trained clergy, would make a difference. How could I tell them that Daddy loved them, Mommy loved them, Jesus loved them, and the preacher loved them, but that Daddy would not be coming home again?

The best thing I could do, I decided, would be to stop at their house every afternoon and play baseball with them. How long, though, would my other obligations allow that?

To make matters worse, I watched helplessly as their mother struggled through a remarriage that failed. As their family life unraveled, those boys became like orphans.

I continued to feel helpless and guilty. I was their pastor. My job was to provide care and meet their needs, was it not?

During those times of feeling inadequate, I would pray, "God, help me! Even if it takes all my life, I've got to find a better solution. My running over to their house for various crises, offering up a blessing, and then driving away, is producing little, if any, lasting good."

Many years later, I am convinced that I have found what was missing. What the boys needed was a community of extended family, akin to those in the frontier days when aunts, uncles, and close, caring neighbors made sure that everything would be in place for the boys to receive the nurture they needed—from hugs and listening ears to baseball gloves and food on the table.

That environment requires not one caregiver but many. For that to happen, the pastor must become a developer, empowerer, and encourager of other caregivers. It took years, but I have made that journey. Is God calling you to do so as well?

The first step in my long journey toward a more whole—and more biblical—perspective was to identify myself as the kind of pastor who is a solo sheepherder and then question whether the way I had applied that role was truly what God calls a pastor to be.

This chapter will, in part, describe myself in my younger years and the literally thousands of fellow sheepherder pastors whom I have observed, counseled with, and researched over the years.

Foundation for the Minister as a Caregiving Coach

The word *pastor* means shepherd or sheepherder, and I do not object to or criticize that role. I am, however, laying the foundation for my conviction that the concept of *pastor* needs a broader, fuller definition than that of solo sheepherder if we are truly to *multiply* disciples, as Jesus commanded in His Great Commission (Matt. 28:19–20).

I will go one step further: maybe the common stereotype of what it means to be a pastor is an imbalanced view. Yes, Jesus does talk about Himself as the Good Shepherd who "calls his own sheep by name" (John 10:3), and who says, "Take care of my sheep" (21:16). Many clergy extrapolate that image to mean that the ideal pastor will know each parishioner personally and be available whenever each one of those sheep has a need.

But that approach to care represents only a portion of the biblical imperative for a church leader and, frankly, may be applicable only to Christ, the one and only Chief Shepherd (1 Pet. 5:4). After all, the only One truly capable of being all-knowing and omnipresent is God.

What about such scriptural terms as *overseer* (Acts 20:28; 1 Tim. 3:2; Titus 1:7) or *leader* (Heb. 13:7, 17)? In the listings of spiritual gifts, can pastors (or shepherds) be endowed by the Holy Spirit with gifts of leadership (Rom. 12:8) or gifts of administration (1 Cor. 12:28)? If so, is there more to or something different in a pastor's role than staying nose to nose with each sheep?

More significantly, what are the pastoral implications of the numerous texts that encourage a mutual "building up" of the body (Eph. 4:12–13, 29; Rom. 15:2; 1 Cor. 3:1–15; 14:12; 2 Cor. 10:8; 13:10; Col. 2:7; 1 Thess. 5:11)? Is it not curious that Paul, in describing pastoral care, uses the image of shepherd only once (Eph. 4:11) and instead employs a wide range of terminology such as *steward of Christ, teacher, example, priest,* and *helmsman?*[1]

How about Jesus's pattern of leadership development (as analyzed in *The Disciple Making Pastor*[2] and elsewhere)? He seemed to spend around three-quarters of His ministry time making other ministers rather than doing the ministry Himself. In my opinion, His approach to "sheep" was much more the model of the rancher or ministry coach than the sheepherder or primary caregiver.

As you read through the following, ask yourself which perspectives best represent the overall teachings of Scripture and the pattern Jesus followed. Also, mull over the implications for size. What correlation do you observe between the leadership style that seems most suited for a numerically plateaued church of fifty and that most suited for a growing church of one hundred?

Push your imagination further by asking what kind of personality is needed to pastor a church of five hundred, one thousand, five thousand, ten thousand, or fifty thousand. If you think these numbers are too high, think of how many unchurched people are within a fifteen-minute drive of your place of worship. What if, through a great awakening akin to other revival periods in American history, these people all began to hunger for spiritual nurture? Would your church be able to service their spiritual needs?

SELF-EVALUATION MOMENT

1. Which words best describe how you feel right now about the concept of pastor as caregiver, coach, and maker of other caregivers: curious, hesitant, confused, a bit defensive, fearful, eager?

2. How do you feel about the biblical underpinnings of the ministry coach idea: intrigued, unconvinced, encouraged, neutral, surprised, reluctant?

How Solo Caregivers Behave

Our field observations indicate that 90 to 95 percent of pastors begin their ministry primarily as solo caregivers. Following are their most common characteristics. Remember, what they do is not wrong; I focus on their behavior, not their hearts.

1. Primary caregiving.

Some pastors try to be the major care providers for the entire church. When they come across a need they ask, "How will *I* meet it?"

When they ask themselves who the adequate caregivers are, they, like Elijah (see 1 Kings 19:14), feel they are probably the only ones, or at least the best ones.

2. Overestimated significance.

The spotlight on their crisis intervention, hospital calls, and other pastoral acts prevents their seeing the supporting roles of other people who are essential to effective care.

It is one thing to tell a church member that her husband has died. It is another for friends and relatives to live with that widow through the years of grieving she needs to surrender her spouse to death.

The true care-heroes in these situations are those who supply the enormous amounts of required aftercare.

3. Expectation drivenness.

Sheepherders attempt to meet all expectations by being omnipresent. They lack discernment, regarding all meetings as crucial, lest they hear the disappointing news, "It just wasn't the same without you" (meaning, "You've created a dependency syndrome").

"What do my people expect of me?" and "Am I measuring up?" are their constant driving motivations. As a result, people set the agenda for the pastors rather than the pastors setting the cadence for the march.

4. Availability.

These ministers think in terms of how they can be more accessible to the church. They convey to the church that they will be available for whatever is necessary.

I remember the first time I heard a pastor refuse to be available for a parishioner's funeral. I thought it an ungodly attitude. He was preaching fifty funerals a year and was headed out for a much-needed vacation with his family. He said, "Although I will not be here for the funeral and cannot come back from the beach, my associate will conduct the funeral in accordance with the departed one's wishes. Let me pray with you before God. I will see you when I return." And he left town.

I thought, *How irresponsible and uncaring can you be?* I was operating on the principle that says, "Even if it means interrupting my vacation I will come back and be here so that your dependence on me will be secured."

Many problems in the parsonage stem from this attitude. Being ever on call means being less available to one's own family. The situation is as if the pastor has a mistress called the church and gives his family only the leftovers. The wife is at a disadvantage in trying to cope with a husband who has these characteristics, unless she also is a sheepherder by disposition.

If she has a different personality, she is likely to feel mad. "If he were literally fooling around on me, I'd confront him," she says. "But what can I do when God or the church is my competition?"

So she is stuck. The choices are to be angry with her husband, be angry with God, or be self-reproachful. The despair sometimes found in the manse stems from a wife who has turned her anger on herself and lives in a brooding condition of self-disrespect, shame, and guilt. (I will expand on this topic in chapter 9.)

5. Performance.

Sheepherders almost seem to think, *How can I keep them from getting along without me?* Although they do not actually verbalize this thought, their behavior indicates it.

Their motto tends to be, "Watch me assure these hospital patients that I'll be back soon." In other words, "Watch me do ministry." (Sadly, much caring ministry is performed without such occasions being used to model for caregivers in training: because no training strategy has been conceived, no one has been invited to come along and observe and share in the caregiving.)

Because their attention is riveted on this solo performance, the strokes they hunger for are linked to their performance standards. They regularly reflect on how the people like their sermons and if the people are pleased with their bedside manner.

6. Role comfort.

Although sheepherders work to the limit of their time and energy, they do not ask for a greater vision than what they can do by themselves. They may be tired, but they are happy: "I'm so grateful to be needed!"

I remember many a time going home dead tired. As I would lie down in bed I would say, "Isn't it wonderful to be this tired and this happy, because I was needed every hour today?"

Never mind that my wife could say, "What about my needs? What about our children's needs? What about the needs of others in the church who haven't been given the chance to develop the same kind of serving skills you so enjoy?"

Sheepherders avoid uncomfortable questions about whether a different path would lead to greater effectiveness.

Years passed before I finally understood the reason behind the incongruence between my perspective, my wife's, and even that of the untapped lay caregivers in our congregation. Much of my activity had stemmed from a need to prove to myself that I was worthy and worthwhile.

Sheepherders experience role comfort when they behave consistently, whether effectively or not. They are comfortable because they live a ritualized life. In their liturgies of economy, efficiency, and consistency, they avoid uncomfortable questions about whether a different path would lead to greater effectiveness.

7. Poor delegating ability.

When sheepherders delegate, they tend to specify methods, not outcomes. If a lay volunteer comes along who is more effectiveness oriented, this person becomes frustrated, because the level of direction is more in terms of how the pastor would do it rather than of measurable outcomes. In addition, sheepherders require constant approval of projects in terms of how something is done rather than what is being done, whether or not such feedback is appropriate or necessary.

Progress becomes bottlenecked because sheepherders fail to fulfill a manager's role; they are too busy keeping the work close to themselves. They attract people who are willing to forward the pastor's agenda rather than contribute their own, such as people who have the gift of helps or of hospitality: "Can I join with you on this, Pastor?" or, "How can I help you, Pastor?"

Pretty soon such pastors lament the fact that nobody is present with skills beyond those of hanging up coats and opening doors.

If these sheepherders do use administratively gifted people, they position them primarily as advisors to themselves: "If you were me, what would you advise that *I* do?" So the advice they hear is usually in keeping with a sheepherder's innocuousness.

8. Poor planning.

If these ministers do plan, it's en route to doing. They are frequently caught in an activity cycle: "Here I am again. By the way, what am I going to do?" They find they are too committed to their processes to be able to achieve their overall goals efficiently or effectively.

Their inadequate planning leads to a shortfall of help that, in turn, leads to their doing ministry by themselves. Caught in such a cycle, they regularly bypass the milestones at which others might join the work.

9. Individualism.

Shepherds tend to see the church as made up of individual members. Thus, rather than visualize ministry through the perspective of a workforce of many teams and groups, they perceive it as something to be negotiated through their relationships with specific persons.

10. Ignorance of trends.

Shepherds also live in the now of experience. Their assessment of how things are going derives more from whether they experienced any disagreeable encounters in the last few hours than from reflection on worship trends, giving patterns, or achievement of church goals.

They do not easily correlate forecasts with needed action. They sit, waiting and watching as changes occur but unaware of their significance, because they are so busy ministering nose to nose with the sheep.

The greatest blind spot of most sheepherders is their lack of a sense of growth history and attendance tracking. Why? For sheepherders to take attendance implies that they might have control of it or responsibility for it.

The sheepherder finds it easier to say, "It's God's business to bless, and if He chooses to bless, fine, and if not, fine."

Did not Jesus also say things like, "Whatever *you* bind on earth will be bound in heaven, and whatever *you* loose on earth will be loosed in heaven" (Matt. 16:19, emphasis added)? Yet sheepherders would rather trade in the unseeable spiritual realities than in the measurable organizational realities.

How Ministry Coaches Behave

By contrast, the pastor as minister maker and ministry coach—or the rancher coordinating many sheepherders—gives greater and more careful attention to organizational needs than to personal and professional needs, as seen in the following characteristics.

1. Emphasis on the big picture.

The pastor as caregiving coach may seem not to need people or may seem to be indifferent to their problems.

In reality, however, pastors as minister-coaches are so concerned about people's needs that they are unwilling to abandon their concerns for the ninety-nine while they search for the one. The coaching of other shepherds, they believe, represents the best way to achieve God's purposes for the entire flock.

These ranchers make sure the flock receives pastoral care in a measurable way, primarily through systems of non-clergy-dependent, mutual self-care.[3] The typical forum for this kind of one-another nurture is a small group of up to a dozen people (to be discussed in chapters 10 through 13).

2. Take-charge competence.

Ministry coaches set expectations much as a band director sets the tempo for each song. This trait particularly shows up in areas of change and confrontation.

For example, suppose a single person in the church is living in an unmarried state with another person. The sheepherder may say, "What am I supposed to do? My board members are so tolerant of sin that they wouldn't assist or back me if I tried to initiate disciplinary measures."

The ministry coach takes a different tack. "Before I attempt to discipline this individual, I'd better get the board in shape. If there's any 'shacking up' going on in their own lives, I'd better have that already worked out so that they can deal credibly with problems like this."

So the ministry coach sets the terms for being on the board. "We're going to pray together, study the Bible together, work together, and obey God together. If this isn't to your liking, then maybe a board role is not the best place of service for you at this church."

106

In short, the ministry coach knows how to put the board through an intense training time to promote their spirituality and leadership skills, so that when they complete their time on the board they can be more effective ministers from that point on.

No pastor can bring about such changes overnight. But improvements will never happen unless the pastor knows how to start calling certain shots.

3. One-another ministry expectation.

These pastors set the expectations that the members of the church will give and receive care among one another. A ministry coach will hold up this standard in such a way that everyone understands this is how they do it.

Churches are partly intentional societies but mostly folk cultures governed by a fabric of unwritten rules and expectations. One steering mechanism in folk cultures is the hero-making that occurs in the process of telling stories (as described in chapter 3). The ministry coach publicly cheers those role models who show the way ministry "ought" to be done. The ministry coach sets up a system of mutual care so that the little "owies," emergency calls, and crises that occur weekly do not prevent him or her from attending to the greater works God wants done.

4. Group focus.

Ministry coaches perceive the church in terms of objectives, groups, and ministry teams. Gatherings call for leaders, and teams need supervisors. Ministry coaches, grasping this concept, view their work not as relationships with individuals but as objectives to be accomplished and a staff to be supervised. Acting like the site manager of a huge construction project, they say, "To get this job done, we need two teams for this and three groups for that."

Therefore, the ministry coach sends people, not one by one—because they would require continual maintenance and nurture—but team by team, so that the teams can keep themselves nurtured, maintained, and high in morale.

Ministry coaches see the church, in other words, in terms of group life. When they find administratively gifted persons, these pastors-as-ranchers use such persons as program organizers rather than simply as advisors to themselves.

Acting like the site manager of a huge construction project, they say, "To get this job done, we need two teams for this and three groups for that."

If they ask, "What would you recommend that I do about this situation?" they do not imply "What should *I* do about it?" but rather "What do you recommend needs to be blessed and done about it?" They know how to change the focus of the work from themselves to the objective of the organization, to be owned by the organization. The ministry coach responds, "That sounds like the prescription we need; we'll implement that. Are you willing to take a part in it? If so, take your prescription and work it out. If not, we'll hand your prescription to someone else who is more available."

5. Flexible supervision.

Ministry coaches delegate work and then supervise others. To be effective they must learn enough flexibility in delegation style to meet the needs of persons willing to receive the assignments.

For example, entrepreneurial personalities need only the go-ahead to do the ministry. They are independent initiative takers. All the ministry coach–type leader has to say is, "Here's how what you're doing supports our vision, here's your access to resources, and here's how we'll know when the job is properly done. Please avoid such and such, and check back with me to report progress at such and such a point."

Other types of people cannot simply take an order and run with it. They have to sit and nurse through a problem and visualize it in the presence of a group of concerned people until they have drawn out all the issues—quality assurances, misgivings, subtleties, and preferences. These kinds of persons often love to sit and plan. They would prefer four hours of planning to one hour of execution. Then they need to come back and celebrate that accomplishment before taking on something new.

If you try to treat both types of people similarly, you will achieve greater success mixing oil and water. I will further address the issue of delegation in chapter 10.

6. Outcome objectives.

Ministry coaches focus on what something will look like when it is complete, not how to get there. They are open to ethical, legitimate ways of getting something done that they themselves have not thought of yet. For the ministry coach, something being "my idea" is not a precondition for the acceptability of the method.

Ministry coaches appreciate those who have appropriate gifts for the position. Whereas the sheepherder appreciates comfort from those with the gifts of helps and hospitality, the coach-as-rancher appreciates the fact that the giftedness of laypeople will be broad enough to do the variety of things God wishes to have done.

7. Large-picture focus.

These pastors screen requests for their services by asking two questions: "Is this the kind of thing our church ought to be doing?" and "By whom should it best be done?"

What if the ministry opportunity seems important, and after all resources have been exhausted it seems the ministry coach will need to become involved? The ministry coach, before jumping in, hesitates and says, "If I'm the one to do it, maybe it shouldn't be done at all."

Everyone in ministry, whatever the style, struggles with passing up an opportunity for fear of missing something that may take the church into the future. But there comes a point in his or her life when the pastor-as-rancher realizes energy must be conserved for what is strategically most important: keeping the entire ranch running smoothly. *If I become distracted by this opportunity, knowing that not all opportunities are necessarily godsends, am I going to be able to do all the other things that need to get done?*

8. Role creation.

Ministry coaches also create roles and fill them, assigning the jobs or delegating them to other people. They know how job maturity affects the type of support needed. In other words, if someone is doing something for the first time and is insecure in the process, that person will need a different kind of attention than one who has done it several times.

Furthermore, ministry coaches will recognize the differences in the types of support needed. Does the person need feedback such as, "You are so gifted. This is going to make the folks at the soup kitchen feel encouraged"? Or is the worker more instructional and task oriented, requiring comments such as, "Here are the techniques you can use"?

Furthermore, as people start jobs they need instructions. Later on they need a little patting. After a while they can get along without instructions if they receive occasional notice. Ultimately, they will do their ministry whether the ministry coach participates or not, because the intrinsic value of the activity is payoff enough for them. Their main concern about the pastor at that point is that he or she not get in their way.

9. Nondependency.

The driving motivation of a ministry coach is how to enable people to function well without the pastor. One of the ministry coach's solutions is to affirm people's talents: "Bless you. You do a great job with that!"

When someone challenges the ministry coach's apparent loss of control, the response is not one of feeling defensive or threatened. "No, this person's willingness to minister means that lives are being touched, even if I am at home getting some much-needed rest." Ministry coaches' freedoms originate in a mental permission note they carry around:

Dear Friend,
   You do not have to carry the burden of the whole world today. That's my job.

                                                                Love,
                                                                God

Ministry coaches refuse to live on the schedule of a nursing mother, who can be away from her baby only so many minutes between feedings and changings. Ministry coaches want their spiritual offspring to grow up—or at least to be nursed by someone else—so they can think, pray, and plan the next hill that the church, as a whole, needs to climb.

10. Managerial skills.

Most pastors have learned managerial talk; few have developed competent managerial behavior. Pulpit ministers, in general, are articulate. They are experts at sounding good. They excel at appearing to be fully adequate.

The reality? When ministers speak of their dreams, I pause at the part that sounds slickest and without hitches. I begin to probe those areas. It often turns out that the more ideal-sounding the plan, the less the minister knows about how to pull it off.

Ministry coaches reserve solitary time for planning and prayer. They make planning a formal, written activity, even if they minister in a context where everything has to be announced orally. They develop skills to sense needs, define problems, and solve problems.

Figure 4

Do You Have a Process for Training and Commissioning New Caregivers?

When to Make the Shift

Can solo caregiving pastors become the kind of leaders who are caregiver, coach, and maker of other caregivers? Frequently, if they really want to. Unless such pastors are convinced that they are fulfilling all God is calling them to become, I urge them to carefully and incrementally revise their behavior in favor of a more effective set of skills, feelings, perceptions, and behaviors.

What about a church that is small? Should the leaders wait to develop pastoral ranching skills until the fellowship shows some growth?

No. For any size church to grow, the leader must address the management issues related to ranching. Otherwise, the church may betray the growth opportunities sent to it.

In almost every case, small-parish pastors think of their churches as smaller than they actually are. They do not realize that the church needs a better organizational scheme or more deliberate supervisory skills.

In preparing a church for growth, the first person to deal with in the chain of change is the minister, because he or she sets up a community of self-reinforcement that either assures nongrowth or permits growth.

Must You Develop Minister-Making Skills?

Some pastors and lay leaders serve churches that, like a puppy, seem to follow them around wherever they go. The people do not attempt much of anything without them. If the leader is not there, everything goes on hold. Both pastor and church find great comfort in the sheepherder role.

Such an experience is not limited to smaller churches. Many people, even in larger churches, are mentally and emotionally back at the level of a lapdog church.[4]

I cannot tell you God's will for your particular situation. Maybe you are already ministering to everyone He wants to bring your way. Maybe the circumstances are such that your context is best served by a sheepherder. As I pointed out in chapter 5, you must make that decision before God.

In counseling with pastors and lay leaders, I find that sometimes their motivation to stay at their present level stems from an unmet need on their part. Some sheepherders enjoy feeling indispensable because of personal workaholism, a need to control others or to be treated like deity to feel good, or a need to be a big fish in a little pond. I will further discuss these tendencies in chapter 9.

Why Ministry Modeling and Coaching Are Significant

What's the bottom line on these two ministry styles? People's need to receive care must exceed your need to give it. If you are to be effective in ministry, you must accept the fact that there will be times when you cannot be both available and adequate.[5]

I suggest that by shifting paradigms pastors or lay leaders can help more people than they would have previously thought possible. In faithfulness to God they say, "We're here as Your instruments of Your gospel, of Your kingdom, of Your body, and we want to do all You are calling us to do in this place."

Therefore, what if God wanted you to handle twice as many people as you are ministering to at present? What if there are people in your church whom God wants to bless, but because you are sticking with a limited way of doing things, you cannot turn those people loose to find God's blessing?

What if God wanted you to handle twice as many people as you are ministering to at present?

I do not believe I have the right to impose a particular growth rate or church size on someone else. But I do believe I have an obligation to encourage pastors and lay leaders to ask God if He might be interested in touching more people than they have previously imagined.

I have yet to be in a place where, from everything I could sense, God was not more willing to bless than the leaders were willing to receive. God wants to give you a spiritually healthy church with a positive, faith-oriented, biblically sound approach to your community, under Christ, such that if someone joins you, he or she will be significantly better off for having done so.

Maybe that means touching ten more people than at present. Or maybe it means ten thousand. Your responsibility is to do whatever you can, humanly speaking, to make spiritual ministry available for "whosoever will."

And, in my opinion, the rancher style is the most effective way to multiply the scope of your ministry.

FOR FURTHER THOUGHT

1. Which sheepherder characteristics describe your ministry style? Which ministry coach or rancher characteristics? How are you different today, in this regard, from the way you were a year ago?

2. In the history of your particular church, would you say the sheepherder style or the rancher style has been more predominant? Why? What factors influence your church either to desire sheepherders or to tolerate ranchers?

3. The section of this chapter titled "Foundation for the Minister as a Caregiving Coach" mentions a number of biblical terms, images, and directives. Which statement is the most eye-opening to you? Which angle would you like to pursue further? Why?

4. Respond to these statements: "What's the bottom line on these two ministry styles? People's need to receive care must exceed your need to give it." "There will be times when you cannot be both available and adequate."

5. If you operated more like a ministry coach, in what ways would your church be different one year from now? Five years from now?

Where Do You Stand on the Spectrum of Care Provider versus Caregiving Coach?

During my early pastoral years, I ministered as if the world's salvation hung on my being available for everyone's primary-care needs. Through my preaching, church-staff supervision, church-school administration, and being on call for twenty-four-hour hospital visitation, I conveyed the idea that I was glad to take care of any situation just as soon as I could get there.

If someone had asked why my ministry was so dependency-centered, I would have responded with a blank stare. I was grateful to be needed! I had a church full of people who viewed me as their shepherd (interpreted as primary caregiver). What greater sign of effectiveness could I want?

Coaching Instead of Doing

One year, however, as I was busy wearing myself out, a certain church member began to out-persist me in hospital visitation. She continually embarrassed me by being at the bedside before I could get there. Each time she gave me a report on her "rounds," I was stung by my inability to effectively cover "my" territory. My feelings of guilt prevented me from seeing how much this woman delighted in her daily search to find and minister to a different sick person.

If this were not enough, another parishioner began handing me prospect cards on all the people she met. She seemed to come across a new person every two hours. My desk at work and dresser at home were soon buried under these cards, and all I could think of was how inadequate I was.

This frustrating overload drove me to ask a strange question. On a particular Sunday, when I saw one of these dear saints walking toward me with news of yet another contact, I became angry at the increased work she generated for me. I looked at her and thought, *What on earth has made you so caring?*

An answer from heaven instantly entered my mind: *I made her that way, so don't you despise what you see.*

If that's what you've done, I shot back to God, *then what am I supposed to do?*

The Lord then impressed me with an idea that I have used ever since. I decided to coach this lady on how to do the ministry by herself or along with another layperson.

"If you were to go for me," I explained when she again recruited me for a new hospital need, "you might select a passage of Scripture, read it, say a prayer for the person, and ask if things are well with his soul." As I continued this impromptu training session, I quickly discovered that she seemed able to learn to present the plan of salvation as capably as I had learned to do.

Even so, I was still terrified as I spoke. I was about to give away a role that most ordained people, including myself, have traditionally insisted on fulfilling themselves. I was giving ministry to an unlicensed and unordained person who had nothing but a love for Jesus, a heart for people, and a willingness to be taught. Could she really pull this off without having as much training as I had? Somehow, I proceeded to encourage and authorize her to do the ministry. As she walked away, I suspected I had unleashed a dynamic that I would understand much better in the years to come.

That event indeed turned out to be pivotal. It was my first step away from a clergy-dependency mind-set and a significant step in applying the directive in Ephesians 4:11–12 for pastors and teachers to equip the *saints* to do the work of the ministry.

Through dozens of similar situations, the Holy Spirit has prompted me to be more effective in directing, managing, and delegating ministry rather than attempting to do it all myself. I have matured in this area step-by-step, in things as little as handing some chalk to a leading board member, sitting down, and letting him use his administrative gifts to chart out a change I had proposed.

Learning is always an ongoing, never-ending process. As the ancient proverbs say: "The heart of the discerning acquires knowledge, for the ears of the wise seek it out," and "Instruct the wise and they will be wiser still; teach the righteous and they will add to their learning" (Prov. 18:15; 9:9).

Your Turn to Coach

Caregiving coaches are not judged only by what they can do themselves. Their value now as a personal care provider is augmented and sometimes overshadowed by what they can get done through others. Their starting point for action, then, is to recognize the potential in taking others along with them and clearly pursuing the training of others.

What does the following checklist reveal about how you invested your ministry hours in recent weeks?

Is a caregiving coach prohibited from doing hands-on ministry? No. That is the privilege of every believer. But wherever possible,

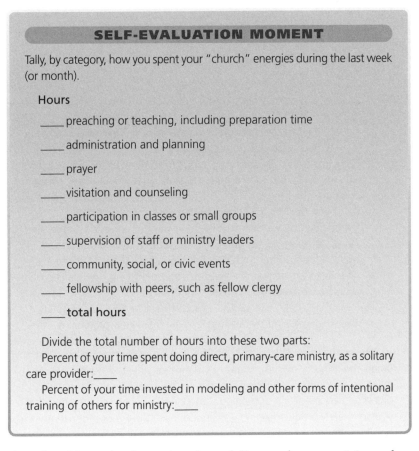

SELF-EVALUATION MOMENT

Tally, by category, how you spent your "church" energies during the last week (or month).

Hours

____ preaching or teaching, including preparation time

____ administration and planning

____ prayer

____ visitation and counseling

____ participation in classes or small groups

____ supervision of staff or ministry leaders

____ community, social, or civic events

____ fellowship with peers, such as fellow clergy

____ **total hours**

Divide the total number of hours into these two parts:
Percent of your time spent doing direct, primary-care ministry, as a solitary care provider:____
Percent of your time invested in modeling and other forms of intentional training of others for ministry:____

that should involve intentional modeling and apprenticing other caregivers. I suggest that one way to measure the effectiveness of paid, professional clergy is to discern what percentage of their hours go to leadership development.

I challenge pastors to be minister developers, and then to measure every other effect in the church by that standard—not by how impressive the sermon is but by how many ministers are made, and not by how available or busy the pastors are but by the extent to which the paid staff contributes to the making of ministers who would care both for the constituency and those beyond the constituency in the name of Jesus Christ.

SELF-EVALUATION MOMENT

What is wrong with these examples? In each, the leader thinks he or she is ranching. Is that the case?

1. "Michelle, how's it going in that Saturday-morning women's group you started?"

   Close. Better: "Michelle, in that new ladies' group you started, have you decided whom to groom as your apprentices?"

2. "Our final topic for staff meeting is special music for this Sunday. Let's ask Kep and Debbie James to sing. They're our most talented musicians. Shall we ask that new trio—Heather, Katie, and Drew—for the next week? Then back to the Jameses for week three?"

   Probably not. Better: "The Jameses are good musicians and able trainers of others. Let's give them the challenge of producing other music leaders, rather than limiting their role to that of performers."

3. "We need an additional minister who could help me oversee our many new programs."

   Maybe. Better: "We need an additional minister who could be responsible for developing lay talent to lead our many new program teams."

The question for a ministry coach to continually reflect on is, "Am I doing the ministry myself, or am I committing others to do it?" I would go so far as to propose that you should not be employed in doing ministry unless you are modeling or training someone else how to do it. Otherwise, you are merely producing care; you are not increasing your production capabilities. Personal caring is legitimate ministry, but it is even better when it is witnessed by someone who is going to take responsibility for doing it next. That principle applies to virtually every activity, from fixing the church photocopier to praying for the flock.

SELF-EVALUATION MOMENT

What does your prayer life reveal about your position on the spectrum of pastor as primary caregiver versus pastor as caregiving coach? What kinds of needs in your flock of church-related people most regularly occupy your prayer times? Check the persons with requests to whom you are most readily drawn:

1. Those whose lives seem to be one crisis after another.
2. Those who have the greatest influence and leadership potential.
3. Those who cause you the most grief.
4. Those who have experienced recent fruit in their ministries.
5. Those with great physical needs.
6. Those who share a passion for developing caregiving leaders.
7. Those parishioners you interact with most frequently, without regard as to whether they play a role in providing care to others.
8. Those with needs you are convinced only you can meet.
9. Those fans whose adoration of your style makes you feel really good.

When one of your parishioners gives you a whole catalog of prayer requests, how are you more likely to respond?
1. "Count on me to support you in prayer."
2. "Do you have your Bible study (or other small group) praying with you?"

Comment: even-numbered answers tend to be ministry coach related; odd-numbered are more characteristic of the primary caregiver.

The Urgency of the Shift

After several decades of careful investigation of the North American church, I have a growing conviction that the way pastors manage themselves as church leaders is the single most important cause for the failure of their churches to perform in the way God requires and in the way the Holy Spirit would empower them to accomplish.

Pastors need enough diagnosis to recognize when they are in trouble and then enough prescription to make a difference when they set their hearts and minds to a new set of priorities.

What is peripheral and what is central? Too many churches lose valuable ministry energy because their leadership is preoccupied with that which is marginal to their mission. Even something as apparently worthwhile as the creation of an in-house training institute that offers an academically oriented, systematic study of the Bible is, in itself, secondary. Knowledge apart from obedient application does not meet the kingdom of God standard of disciples who make disciples.

What, then, is essential? Those activities that organize a pastor's time and vision around a system of lay leadership development, so that greater ministry can be accomplished in ever-widening circles of influence.

The implications are staggering. If the net result will be that most churches need far fewer speakers and far more shepherds of the flock, then the caregiving coach-pastor will need to rethink the role of the vast majority of a church's meetings. Likewise, the prevalent didactic model for judging ministry will be deemed inappropriate. The current stroking-and-reward patterns—number of sermons downloaded, number of radio or TV listeners—will prove to be almost irrelevant ways to keep score.

> Knowledge apart from obedient application does not meet the kingdom of God standard of disciples who make disciples.

A caregiving coach helps a church to state a goal or a mission statement that is in keeping with the commands of Christ to love God, to love one another, and to make disciples (see Matt. 22:37–40; 28:18–20). Then, having stated that goal, the ministry coach will flesh it out in terms of behaviors and programs that are appropriate to the local situation, offering to be a modeler of ministry rather than the person who does the ministry single-handedly.

The caregiving coach seeks out opportunities to empower others and applauds the expansion of caregiving. The desired objective is not less care but assured care.

Yes, pastors and staff are permitted to offer personally provided one-on-one care, but they will do so with the primary intent of equipping additional ministers—volunteers and staff members alike—to do the legitimate work of providing primary care and spiritual nurture to those in need, both within the church constituency and beyond.

> The caregiving coach seeks out opportunities to empower others and applauds the expansion of caregiving.

When this goal becomes more important than the satisfaction of the minister, a church will be able to move beyond single-pastor ministry to multiple-pastor ministry—and in so doing enlarge the flock. Such is the kind of self-management of a leader that can make a most critical difference.

SELF-EVALUATION MOMENT

You and your family are on vacation, and you receive a message at your motel to phone somebody in the church whose name and number you do not recognize. As you receive this news, what is your attitude?

1. I knew I shouldn't go on vacation. They need me!
2. I wish my family could be a little more self-sacrificing. If we'd deny ourselves more, such as not being gone so long on this vacation, we'd have more time for ministry.
3. My family won't mind if we delay our outing so that I can return this call.
4. If it's a real emergency, I'm sure they'll contact this week's deacon on call, who will handle it just fine.
5. I can't believe the secretary or elders released our vacation phone number to anyone other than our key leadership! I'd better give them more training in not allowing themselves to be so dependent on me, and making sure our care team is fully prepared and eager to be on call.

Comment: if interpreted from a care-centered motivation, the higher the number, the more you demonstrated rancher characteristics.

FOR FURTHER THOUGHT

1. The opening paragraph of this chapter contains this confession: "I ministered as if the world's salvation hung on my being available for everyone's primary-care needs." What Scriptures would support that perspective? What passages would challenge it?

2. What are some of your experiences in giving away ministry? How did you feel? How did people respond? What insights have you gained?

3. How do you feel about this statement: "One way to distinguish the activities of paid, professional clergy is by the fact that the vast majority of their hours go to leadership development." What is the reasoning behind this view? What would be the most widespread objection to it?

4. Which self-evaluation moment in this chapter gave you the greatest insight about yourself? On a scale of one to ten, with one being a consummate primary caregiver and ten being a full-scale ministry coach, where do you stand? Why?

Should You Use More Than One Leadership Style?

This chapter helps you provide leadership that your people can follow and helps you discover how different folks need different strokes in how you lead them.

How would the following business advice apply to your church? *When wooing prospects, always remember your existing shareholders. If you focus so heavily on servicing new prospects that you have no money left over to pay dividends, the stock owners will take away your privilege of researching new-customer interests.*

At issue is a principle called stakeholder symmetry, which any effective leader must understand, whether in the business world or the church.

This concept says that every organization includes a huge contingent of people called stakeholders—those with an investment in what you are doing. They care very deeply that in your enthusiastic pursuit of the organization's future you do not forget the powerful contingent who helped create the past.

If, in reaching for what could be, you allow the balance scales to tip too far, you will lose the loyalty of those who treasure what has been.

Suppose you decide, for example, that your Sunday school could be replaced with a program better designed to meet the needs of the population segment your church is targeting. Suppose, further, that those now participating in your Sunday school oppose your plan. If you are not careful, you may find that while you paddle forward toward your version of a preferred future, your Sunday school people will drop stones in your canoe.

While you push forward with those willing to explore new things, watch out that certain partisan groups do not sink you.

Stakeholder symmetry offers this warning: while you push forward with those willing to explore new things, watch out that certain partisan groups do not sink you.

Almost every person, in every church, is party to a special interest. One crowd may have a deep concern about your church building, another about your Christian day school or youth group, another about foreign missions, and yet another about denominational issues or even secular politics.

As you lay plans for the future, you would be wise to take all your interest groups into account. Otherwise, any who feel left out or alienated may, as soon as they can find the opportunity, defeat your overall progress.

Who Are Your Stakeholders?

How do you identify your church's multiple constituencies or stakeholder groups? First, realize that some will be insiders, such as staff, choir members, board members, Sunday school people, youth, day-school leaders, and so forth. Others may be outsiders, such as neighbors in whose yards your members park, city officials who fear your vote, denominational officials hoping for a budgetary contribution, and the like. All these people hold an interest in the church you serve and its operation.

Also, do not overlook the invisible realm. It is fully appropriate to identify God both as owner and stakeholder in the progress of His church. After all, Scripture likens the church to the bride of Christ (Eph. 5:25–32; Rev. 22:17), the body of Christ (Rom. 12:4–8; 1 Cor. 12:12–27; Col. 1:18), the family of God (Gal. 6:10; Heb. 2:11; 1 Pet. 4:17), and many other relationships of united purpose.

In opposition to God and His angels are the devil and other evil principalities. Their stake in your church is to thwart your advances. Sadly, in most churches the prevailing culture has become so naturalistic that believers are unaware of the degree to which evil is active. What St. Paul describes as the "fiery darts" of the evil one has been read so figuratively that many who are afflicted with pain and fear in their bodies do not think to rebuke evil in the authority of our Lord Jesus Christ and instead reach for the aspirin bottle. Family feuds and church fights are fueled by unrecognized impulses that arise from lies and objections in the minds of members who do not recognize the difference between their own thoughts, those given by the Holy Spirit, or those implanted in their consciousness by evil.

Second, remember that stakeholders have the ability to make choices regarding the resources they control, whether tangible things such as money or interpersonal influences such as the ability to give or withhold permission. Their participation or boycott is based on their own agendas, purposes, and goals, which may or may not be in agreement with what you are trying to do.

Third, be aware of the significance of the relationship between one stakeholder and another. For example, a coalition may form between nongrowth-minded city officials and taxpayers whose homes neighbor the church properties. They may form a powerful network to oppose the expansion of the church's parking lot. In this case their vested interest affects the outcome of your organization's growth, even if it is only to resist your encroachment on their way of life.

Figure 5

The Berry Bucket Theory

Older Newcomers
(Senior Newberries)

• Suggest
• Show homework

Younger Newcomers
(Junior Newberries)

• Make appropriate suggestions
• Expect to be followed

*See pastor
as "leader" or
commander*

some follow pastor

some side with elders

Polarization Potential

*See pastor as
"chaplain" or
hired hand*

• Ask permission
• Provide leadership to
their agenda

Older Longtermers
(Senior Formerberries)

• Bring reform without alienating
other groups

Younger Longtermers
(Junior Formerberries)

128

A New Slant on Berry Buckets

If there is any one stakeholder issue that most frequently causes grief in churches, it stems from a combination of age and tenure factors. This problem, more than any other I have observed, is a major dynamic in pastoral dismissals and church splits. I summarize the principles of the problem by calling it the "berry bucket" theory of church leadership.[1]

The image is this: in the root cellar of my uncle's farm was a two-shelf storage space for berries gathered from his garden. He dated the berries, as they awaited further processing, by placing yesterday's pick on the bottom shelf and today's pick on the top.

Churches are like root cellars in the sense that they tend to store the "crops" of members in different identifiable clusters. On the bottom shelf is the older guard, and on the top shelf is the newer crowd.

The distinguishing factor is the tenure of the present senior pastor. Those on the bottom shelf, who have been at the church longer than the pastor, are "formerberries." The "newberries," on the top shelf, are those drawn to the church since the present pastor's arrival. One further distinction: those *younger* than the pastor are either "*junior* formerberries" or "*junior* newberries," and those *older* than the pastor are "*senior* formerberries" or "*senior* newberries."

What help does this classification system offer? Each of these four groups has a different perception of the pastor's role. Each group, in turn, requires a different leadership style (see Figure 5).

By recognizing that there are basically four "buckets" represented in a typical church, a pastor can learn to perceive the dissimilar expectations each group brings. In so doing the pastor can anticipate much church conflict and nip it in the bud.

Here is how each of these groups would view you if you were their senior pastor.

129

1. *Junior newberries.*

The easiest people to lead are the junior newberries. They are younger than you and they came to the church after you. Therefore, they tend to take your word about life experiences (you're probably "ahead" of them) and about what happened earlier in the church (they weren't there, but you were). They almost have no choice but to be influenced by you.

Junior newberries perceive you as their leader or even as commanding officer. In most cases, all you need do for them to follow you is to announce where you are going and then to lead the charge.

A forty-two-year-old minister, for instance, will find that the people most excited about joining the church will be, in most cases, in the thirty-five to forty age range. In other words, most pastors find it easiest to win people two to ten years younger than themselves.

2. *Senior newberries.*

Those parishioners who are older than their pastor may respect his or her judgment in some areas, but because they have "been around" longer, they withhold judgment on other issues.

For example, if I join a church led by a young pastor fresh out of seminary, I can buy his enthusiasm for marriage and his excitement about his young family. When it comes to his advice on how to handle my teenage kids, however, I will hear him out but probably not accept it with full credibility.

My wife and I have six children. After going through the teenage years six times, I am quick to spot simplistic or unrealistic statements about parenting teens. A younger pastor simply has not experienced the life stages of people like me who are twenty or more years his senior.

How do pastors work with senior newberries? They suggest what they would like to see done, they present their rationale and research, and they invite their senior newberries to follow along.

Pastors cannot automatically expect to be trusted until they can show their homework. Why? Senior newberries have lived long enough to see leaders behave foolishly. They will not follow their pastor until they are convinced that he or she is acting with wisdom.

3. Senior formerberries.

The hardest people to lead are those who were part of the church before you came and who are also older than you. Although they may belong to the group that called you to lead their church, that is not what they really want you to do.

Rather, they probably think they hired you to stand in their pulpit, lead the worship service, preach, help them raise their budget, handle weddings and funerals, and visit them in the hospital. In short, they frequently view the pastor as a chaplain or hired hand. Or they have a long history of having led different initiatives in the church, and they expect their new pastor to let them help lead and probably shape how that's done.

Senior formerberries cannot be led in the same way as junior newberries. You lead the younger group by suggestion and excitement—by a dream appropriate to you in your present tenure at church and your life stage. They accept it because they like you and can identify with your vision. But the group who preceded you had all kinds of ideas before you came. You represented only a part of their ideal for their future. You were the best fit they could find.

To provide leadership to senior formerberries, you need to listen carefully as you ask them, "What do you think God is calling this church to do and be? What direction are we heading? Where are we going? What are we doing? How do you want to help?"

Then provide leadership for them to reach *their* objectives. As you empower their dreams, they will increasingly trust—and permit—your leadership to reach the rest of the church.

131

Or, to restate it humorously, the minister's modus operandi goes like this: "I am their leader so I *follow* them. As soon as I find out where they want to go, I'll stand at the head of the line so I don't look bad."

I would add: do not get too far ahead of that line or you will turn around and not find them. Instead, stay close enough that you can know when they turn, and then change course with them.

Young pastors often have a hard time with this perspective, because it may be alien to their dreams of exerting power. There is a difference between leading and providing leadership, however. Or, to repeat one unknown wit, the difference between a leader and a martyr is about three paces.

The longer you are in the church, the more trust you earn from senior formerberries and the more the church's vision will unify around your personal vision.

Are there any exceptions? One involves founding pastors. In some ways no one can "outformerberry" them, because no one was there ahead of them. Church-planting pastors, therefore, frequently do not have to deal with as many permission issues as clergy in established churches.

Lyle Schaller pointed out another important exception. Some long-established mainline churches seem dead in the water. When you ask where they are going, the people indicate that what they are best at is sitting. Schaller says their primary agenda is to avoid getting very deeply involved. His advice to pastors is, "Don't try to outpassive the passive." In other words, try to stay connected with the church, keep loving them, but also set before them some goals consistent with what they are capable of accomplishing. In the process, coax them to become more active.[2]

4. Junior formerberries.

These are usually the children of the senior formerberries. They are the hardest group to peg, because sometimes they accept the view of their elders (the senior formerberries) and sometimes they side with newcomers to the church (the newberries).

Avoiding Forced Terminations and Schisms

Pastors soon discover that these four types of people are not led with equal ease. Each needs a different set of signals.

Pastors frequently observe the greatest polarization between only two of these groups: the senior formerberries and the junior newberries. These two "buckets" are usually the most distinct from each other in both identity and leadership needs.

Further, a minister who has been at a church for a while can easily develop quite a substantial following of newberries. In many cases, he or she will attract several newberries for each formerberry present. This circumstance often results in the pastor concentrating attention on the newer blood.

The usual next stage in this progression is that the pastor fails to give leadership to both groups. The older guard becomes more or less ignored. Leadership, by default, goes to the junior newberries. After all, they represent a sizable percentage of the church and they are excited about both their minister and their church.

But in the process, who feels neglected and has their feelings hurt? Senior formerberries. Who, in turn, has the greatest ability to hurt the pastor? In most cases, senior formerberries.

This kind of strained relationship is often at the root of forced terminations and church splits. Senior formerberries tend to control most of the keys: to the church kitchen, to the church vehicles, to the treasury, and to the boardroom. That spells *clout*.

Pastors must think of themselves not as leaders of one big church family but as leaders of groups within the whole who give leadership cues appropriate to the level of need of the persons who require it.

Far better, then, to learn how to employ different leadership styles. Doing so may involve wearing two, three, or four hats a day. With each berry bucket the pastor thinks, *Which hat do I have on now? Am I able to assume the followership of the junior newberries? Am I being a patient chaplain to the senior formerberries? Am I doing enough to show my homework to the junior formerberries?*

Sometimes the minister becomes confused and cries out, "Who am *I*?" It may take time, but a skilled leader can learn how to keep these differing leadership-style hats close at hand and to switch them appropriately.

> Pastors must think of themselves not as leaders of one big church family but as leaders of groups within the whole.

An important "berry bucket" takeaway is that it's neither inauthentic nor inappropriate to shape your communication posture to provide the various constituencies in your congregation the kinds of information and processing they need to be cooperative followers. Such role flexibility contributes to the effectiveness of a caregiving coach.

FOR FURTHER THOUGHT

1. Do you agree with the berry bucket concept of a church's composition and of the leader wearing different hats when working with different groups? Why or why not?

2. Who are the main stakeholder groups within your church? Outside your church?

3. In what ways is stakeholder symmetry at work among your parishioners? Who are the chief senior formerberries? The chief junior newberries? If there is friction between these groups at present, what does church leadership need to do to help them work together?

4. What is the relationship between the leader's skill at role flexibility and the breaking of a church's growth barriers?

Multiply by Releasing

Have you ever asked yourself, *What is feeding my limitations?* Or more bluntly, *To what extent am I the limiting factor?*

As church leaders try to develop more effective leadership skills, they sometimes discover that one of their greatest obstacles is themselves—in particular, their own unresolved personal and family issues.

Recovery and development are a lifelong process. I myself am a product of a family marked by several generations of deep pain. The way I compensated for it followed the same path many Christians have taken: I became a workaholic.

I hid from my pain in endless work. I have often put in unsustainable seventy-hour weeks. When I could not accomplish enough work during the daytime, I would put my family to bed, get up in the middle of the night, and work some more. My wife often said, and rightly so, that I would rather work than sleep.

I am a driven man. As a result, I have difficulty feeling like a worthy person if I am not putting in those impossible hours. I once set a target of working only sixty hours a week, as a first step of progress. But that took so much work that I became exhausted.

Through insights I gained from the twelve-step recovery movement and teachings about family dysfunction, I became aware that my workaholism was causing serious repercussions.

I remember how I would come home at night after a fourteen-hour day of pastoring a growing church and managing our church's Christian day school, which was the largest private school in our region. I would unload my pockets onto the bedroom dresser and find a note about a death call at the hospital, or a critically ill patient, or something similar, and feel I had to go back out and deal with it personally.

Why did I think that working inordinate hours, pushing myself to the point of fatigue and sickness, was truly honoring to God? Who was I trying to impress? What kind of fatherly and husbandly duties was I avoiding by working so much?

My recovery began the day I repented of this self-deception. I am now a recovering workaholic—with a long way to go. I have lost more battles than I have won, but at least I am not kidding myself as much, anymore.

The principle, which can apply to any pastor or layperson, is this: a surprising amount of our struggle to be leaders comes from misguided notions about ourselves and our need to do ministry when, in fact, God would be far more pleased if we would see that ministry get done.

Sometimes the matter is merely one of well-intended but nonetheless nonstrategic priorities. For me it was an issue of telling myself something that was not true. Not every care need needed to be fulfilled by me.

Ministry fatigue is not God's gift to church leaders. Rather, one of its sources can be traced to the consequence of self-deceit, with the result that we work harder instead of smarter. Anyone who takes this concept to heart will have made a major step toward revising his or her life and goals as a manager and leader.

God is willing to forgive me. But He also wants me to pursue an alternate route so I do not fall into the same trap again.

Take a Deacon Next Time

What could I have done when I unloaded my pockets and found that message about a hospital call? Why not phone one of our church's deacons, elders, prayer ministry leaders, or other trained caregivers? If any of God's people have been gifted and equipped to serve in these ways, then I should call, whether it seemed to be a convenient time or not.

If I always had an apprentice present, my overload would not have lasted long.

Suppose I contacted Mario. The first time we would go together to the hospital. He would observe me, join with me in caring, and then debrief with me afterward. Maybe he and I would do that one more time with someone else in need. The next time he could go without me. Ideally, soon he would bring another deacon to train. And I would see that they were both applauded as champions.

If, in working seventy hours in a week, I always had an apprentice present, my overload would not have lasted long. Why? There would be so many apprentices who wanted to work that they would have gobbled up much of the primary-care ministry I was trying to do.

The Church Leader's Personal Life

What about other ministry frustrations and pressures that clergy and active lay leaders face? Could some of them likewise be rooted in dysfunctional habits? How many issues in the typical leader's personal life stem from unrecognized self-deception?

Take, for example, the motivation of saving face. How much leadership behavior is driven by a need to look good in front of others? How many ministers' wives, out of fear of being criticized for not supporting their husbands, never ask themselves, *What do I want?* Instead they behave codependently toward their church, allowing the question, "What does the congregation want?" to control their every decision.[1] How many pastoral couples are so dominated by a need to maintain a pretense that they cover up their times of need when things are not faring well with their marriage or children?

Suppose the pastor of your church has a wife and small children. Would there ever be a time when he could say the following without feeling guilty or projecting blame? "No, my wife is at home, and she probably won't be here Sunday, either. She's exhausted, and we've neglected our kids recently, and the way I've set expectations that we will always be willing and able to give care personally means that her only chance for recovering with some quiet family time is when you're here at the church building meeting with me!"

Or consider the idea of a church as an addictive organization. The book *The Subtle Power of Spiritual Abuse* relates the true account of a young pastor who said to his board, "I'm really hurting. Our family is not being spiritually fed, we're not surviving on our sustenance budget, we can't pay our bills, and the stress is unbelievable."

The chairman of the board responded, "Pastor, I rule you out of order; you're not on the agenda." This story shows a pastor who was finally willing to say, "Help!" The unfortunate response implied, "You can't get well. If you do, our sickness will show up too. Therefore, that's not to be discussed here."[2]

In this story it seems that the scoundrel was the board member. Had I cited another true case study, which reversed the roles, the fault could seem to rest with the pastor. But in reality, no person is the real culprit. The villain is a system, and everyone in it can become victim to it.

More Are Addicts Than Acknowledge It

We could examine any number of topics, from adrenaline addiction to resentment in the parsonage or in the home of an active layperson. The relevant lesson from the recovery community is that the problems seen in the drunk are not confined to people who abuse alcohol. Our bodies create excitements that behave like alcohol in that they preoccupy us and drive our feelings. The net result is that many more of us are addicted than go around wearing the badge.

I find in my work with churches that the first thing to collapse on the road to addiction is people's clear view of themselves. It is almost as if they look in the mirror and see not themselves but a picture of a perfected self, one free from all addiction. With this loss of perspective the progression can continue until they become blind even to the feedback of those who are in a position to tell them the truth, especially their intimates. Finally they lose their ability to balance work and home life.

As alienation grows within their families, their flight from intimacy creates two hideous consequences. First, they lose their spirituality, the ability to feel toward God and to respond to the pricks of conscience. The insides of their souls feel flatlined. No quickening at the mention of the name of God. No looking forward to a time of solitude in prayer. Pursued by the hound of heaven, they race onward in their frantic business. Addicts hope that somehow God will catch up with them. At the same time, they are terrified to allow Him to come close.

Second, they can lose their personal morality. "But how can I lose my personal morality," asks the Christian who has the addiction, "if I'm faithful to my spouse? I couldn't even be accused of flirting!" The sleeping around that catches so much press attention is often a suicidal cry. It traces back to desperate pastors who have lost their way and decided to end it all. They cannot build up the nerve to drive off

The first thing to collapse on the road to addiction is people's clear view of themselves.

a cliff, so they take an intern or attractive staff member to a motel and symbolically do the same thing by jumping off a moral cliff.

Addicts lose their personal morality by two lies. First is the falsehood of denial when they assert, "I don't have a problem." Then, more insidiously, they lie to protect their supply of addictive substance. Pornography addicts stash their girlie magazines, alcoholics cover up their whiskey cache, and church leaders, if they are workaholics, protect their supply of work. To them, work is righteous, work is right, work is what God expects, work is an escape from the evils of humanity, and work is a deliverer from dealing with problems at home.

Are workaholics not too busy working to have time to create lies? How do they protect their supply of addictive substance? With a little voice that whispers, as they unpack their pockets and find a reminder of an unfinished need, *The sacrifice will be worth it, because this is what God called me to do.*

That response, for the workaholic, is a lie if he or she thinks, *It's okay to neglect my family*, or *No one else can do the job as well*, or *Only I am willing to make the necessary sacrifices to meet this need.*

For a while, spouses or children may protest. In most cases, though, they gradually surrender and behave codependently themselves. "Well, if it's the work of God, then I guess we'll have to help you do it." They learn that survival means cooperating with the family lie.

Whether or not the family cooperates, the workaholic is unavailable to them emotionally because of preoccupation with his or her work. As a result, the family members, constantly reaching for approval and emotional security, develop self-image problems. The hole in their souls leads them to a lifestyle of wanting to help too much. That quest may fulfill itself in their choosing codependent spouses or codependent careers. Their messianic drive says, *I, and only I, can make a difference in all of those people's lives.*

The person who feels the greatest trap is usually the pastoral spouse, especially if that person is a woman who devotes great energy to supporting her husband's ministry. This clergy spouse often has enormous feelings of both inadequacy and anger. Worse, she feels a second damnation because she decides that her emotions are unspiritual, an outlook that only adds to her despondency. She has given up her heart and life, her body and mind, and now finds herself unable to complain through her pain.

Grabbing On to Hope

The time has come when many people are blowing the whistle. From Christian psychologists to veteran pastors, a rally cry is going out: "Now that we've finally defined workaholism and other forms of addiction and codependency as a mismanagement of ministry, let's not tolerate it one minute longer!"

What is recovery about? Its theological roots grow in the rich soil of God's grace. God reconciles us to Himself and renews us day by day, not by our good works but by His riches in Christ Jesus (2 Cor. 5:17–21; Eph. 2:4–10; Phil. 4:12–13).

That grace creates the solid living hope described in many Scripture passages, such as 1 Peter 1:3–9, and affirmed in this prayer of the ancient church: "Although man lost the friendship of God through sin, God has offered covenants to man, and God's prophets have taught mankind to hope for salvation."[3]

We addicts have hope because God gives us salvation: not only life with Him in heaven but deliverance for here and now as we are freed from our addictive lies. Repentance of sin truly leads to wholeness.

Read the Twelve Steps from Alcoholics Anonymous (with only slight modification for Christian purposes, as noted by the brackets), which offer a liturgy for dealing with sin.

1. We admitted we were powerless over (name the [sin])—that our lives had become unmanageable.
2. We came to believe that a power [Jesus Christ], greater than ourselves, could restore us to sanity.

3. We made a decision to turn our will and our lives over to the care of God, as we understood Him.

4. We made a searching and fearless moral inventory of ourselves.

5. We admitted to God, to ourselves, and to another human being the exact nature of our wrongs.

6. We became entirely ready to have God remove all these defects of character.

7. We humbly asked Him to remove our shortcomings.

8. We made a list of all persons we have harmed, and became willing to make amends to them all.

9. We have made direct amends to such people whenever possible, except when to do so would injure them or others.

10. We continued to take personal inventory, and when we are wrong promptly admitted it.

11. We sought through prayer and meditation to improve our conscious contact with God as we understood Him, praying only for the knowledge of His will for us and the power to carry that out.

12. And, having had a spiritual awakening as a result of these steps, we tried to carry this message to [those Jesus brings our way], and to practice these principles in all our affairs.[4]

This list is a life preserver for people drowning in a storm. It is for people desperately trying to find the love, grace, and companionship of God. Even though many Christians, including myself, have serious reservations about some of the things taught by the twelve-step movement, this more than any other approach I know helps addicts deal forthrightly with their sin.

Availing oneself of group support is a critical component, because most of us do not have either the clarity of sight about ourselves or the developed disciplines needed to follow through on the process of recovery. Most of us need to come alongside other sympathetic people who will say, "You're not slipping back into those old patterns, are you?" or "It appears that you're falling into those old patterns. What are you going to do so that you won't have more to confess next week than you do this week?"

In the twelve-step community, the people who have made the most progress have done so through sponsorship. Someone was willing to be intimately involved in their process of recovery and say, when needed, "Cut the self-deception. You are slipping and you know it. I can smell it, you can feel it, and anybody who is close to you knows it. Now stop it. What is driving you to do this? Let's deal with it!"

How many times someone falls off the wagon is immaterial. Jesus said to Simon Peter, "Simon, you're going to betray me." He answered, "No, not me, Lord." "Yes," Jesus said. "You will betray me. I'm praying for you that after you have recovered, you will strengthen your brethren" (see Luke 22:31–34).

Listening to God

What do Christian addicts need to hear? I believe God wants to say, "My daughter or son, I have everything under control. Sit in My lap a little longer, because after you leave Me, what's going to happen next will endure only if it's in line with what I'm doing. Everything else will perish. More than filling your mind with information or driving your body to accomplish programs, you need to learn to live in My love. Abide in Me."

Would such a perspective encourage people to give less of themselves to the Lord's work? Would it hamper someone's obedience to Jesus's command to "take up their cross daily and follow me" (Luke 9:23)? No; it would achieve just the opposite. The wholeness I describe will motivate people to serve God as Jesus did—not with anger but with joy (John 15:11; Heb. 12:2), and not with a drive to be accepted but with good works motivated by God's tremendous grace (Eph. 2:8–10).

143

> *I see the day coming when the Western church will be known as the place that offers health.*

I see the day coming when the Western church will be known as the place that offers health. Church leaders will know how to give permission for people to develop relational ministry, and the caring, nurturing groups of strugglers who have found bread in the presence of Jesus Christ will invite others to their table. Forgiveness, healing, and deliverance from addictive sin will be multiplied across the face of this continent.

Let us leaders set the pace by personally participating in such a community, being willing to let down the barriers, and speaking with candor of our own human and spiritual needs. Let us forge ahead and create such communities where they do not now exist.

Over the last twenty years we have watched Saddleback's Celebrate Recovery and other Christ-centered recovery programs bring freedom and wholeness. May they increase!

FOR FURTHER THOUGHT

1. Where do you personally identify most with Carl's personal story in this chapter?

2. How many pastors or heavily involved laypeople do you know who struggle with workaholism? For the person you know who is the most recovered, what pathway did God use?

3. What message would God say to you about your own addictive behaviors? If He were to use a Scripture text, which would He emphasize to you?

4. What is the relationship between a leader overcoming workaholism (or another addictive behavior) and the breaking of a church's growth barriers?

PART 3

BREAK SPECIFIC GROWTH BARRIERS

How to Break the 200 Barrier

This chapter begins with a number of assumptions. Most fundamentally, it trusts that at the heart of your mission is the life-changing good news that Jesus Christ came to seek and to save the lost (Luke 19:10). It counts on your church's leadership having both a vision for disciple-making growth and a commitment to it (Matt. 28:19–20).[1] It supposes that you do *not* want to communicate to your visitors that your church's identity is tied to remaining at your present size. It also presumes that your church knows how to attract newcomers and thus draws a flow (or trickle) of first-time guests.[2]

It further assumes that you are willing to modify your leadership style in ways that encourage growth. One essential ingredient is the shift from pastor as sheepherder or primary caregiver to pastor as caregiver, ministry coach, and maker of other caregivers.

In short, I am writing to people who are experiencing personal spiritual renewal, whose churches are beginning to reap a harvest, and who want additional resources and biblically based advice for making the most of their ministry potential.

Your New Peer Group

Through hundreds of consultations and thousands of pastoral surveys we have learned something very significant: churches have more in common by their size than by their denomination, tradition, location, age, or any other single, isolatable factor.[3]

In other words, leaders ministering in a church with a weekend worship attendance (adults and children)[4] of 200 will develop a sense of camaraderie far more quickly and naturally with leaders from another church of the *same* size, even if from a different denomination or tradition, than they will with colleagues from their communion who represent a church larger or smaller than themselves.

> Churches have more in common by their size than by their denomination, tradition, location, age, or any other single, isolatable factor.

The typical church in North America is small. Half of this continent's approximately 320,000 Protestant churches[5] run about 80 in weekly attendance.[6]

When your church breaks through 100 in its regular attendance, you as pastor or key lay leader may begin to ask yourself, *Am I wrong to have started to see things differently from most of my ministry colleagues?*

The answer is no. In trying to find some wisdom appropriate to your next step of growth, you are discovering that your peers, for the most part, have not had to deal with certain questions and issues you are now facing.

At the 100 mark in attendance, your church has become larger than 60 percent of your peers'; at 140, 75 percent; at 200, 85 percent; at 350, 93 percent; and by 500, 95 percent. At 1,000 you hit the 99th percentile. When your average attendance climbs beyond 2,000 (99.5th percentile), your identity is so distinct that this chapter could list every such North American church by name.[7] At about 8,000 you enter the ranks of the "100 Largest Churches" in North America (see also Figure 6).[8]

148

Figure 6

Which Group Represents Your Church's Attendance, and Where Will Your Next Growth Steps Take You?

Examples of America's weekly worship attendance by church size
(all services, adults and children)

45% of all surveyed churches have an attendance of 50 or less

Worship Attendance of 50 or Less
(number and percent of each denomination's churches)

Denomination	Number
Methodist (UMC)	17,794
American Baptist	796
Presbyterian (PCUSA)	3,588
Nazarene	2,113
Episcopal	2,860
Wesleyan	696
Southern Baptist	15,242
Assemblies of God	4,511
Lutheran (ELCA)	3,366
Alliance (C&MA)	591

0% 10% 20% 30% 40% 50%

61% of all surveyed churches have an attendance of 75 or less (16% have attendance of 51-75)

Worship Attendance of 51–75
(number and percent of each denomination's churches)

Denomination	Number
American Baptist	336
Lutheran (ELCA)	1,707
Wesleyan	290
Nazarene	804
Alliance (C&MA)	321
Southern Baptist	6,671
Assemblies of God	1,963
Presbyterian (PCUSA)	1,173
Episcopal	1,028
Methodist (UMC)	4,547

0% 5% 10% 15% 20%

88% of all surveyed churches have an attendance of 200 or less (27% have attendance of 76-200)

Worship Attendance of 76–200
(number and percent of each denomination's churches)

Denomination	Number
Alliance (C&MA)	648
Lutheran (ELCA)	3,171
American Baptist	495
Episcopal	2,001
Assemblies of God	3,556
Southern Baptist	11,548
Nazarene	1,215
Wesleyan	418
Presbyterian (PCUSA)	1,849
Methodist (UMC)	6,638

0% 10% 20% 30%

95% of all surveyed churches have an attendance of 350 or less (7% have attendance of 201-350)

Worship Attendance of 201–350
(number and percent of each denomination's churches)

Denomination	Number
Alliance (C&MA)	164
Assemblies of God	910
Lutheran (ELCA)	753
Southern Baptist	2,947
Episcopal	473
Wesleyan	111
American Baptist	90
Nazarene	284
Presbyterian (PCUSA)	438
Methodist (UMC)	1,697

0% 5% 10%

continued next page

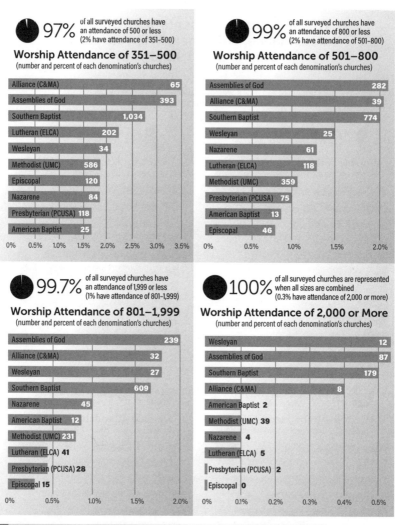

97% of all surveyed churches have an attendance of 500 or less (2% have attendance of 351–500)

Worship Attendance of 351–500
(number and percent of each denomination's churches)

Alliance (C&MA)	65
Assemblies of God	393
Southern Baptist	1,034
Lutheran (ELCA)	202
Wesleyan	34
Methodist (UMC)	586
Episcopal	120
Nazarene	84
Presbyterian (PCUSA)	118
American Baptist	25

0% 0.5% 1.0% 1.5% 2.0% 2.5% 3.0% 3.5%

99% of all surveyed churches have an attendance of 800 or less (2% have attendance of 501–800)

Worship Attendance of 501–800
(number and percent of each denomination's churches)

Assemblies of God	282
Alliance (C&MA)	39
Southern Baptist	774
Wesleyan	25
Nazarene	61
Lutheran (ELCA)	118
Methodist (UMC)	359
Presbyterian (PCUSA)	75
American Baptist	13
Episcopal	46

0% 0.5% 1.0% 1.5% 2.0%

99.7% of all surveyed churches have an attendance of 1,999 or less (1% have attendance of 801–1,999)

Worship Attendance of 801–1,999
(number and percent of each denomination's churches)

Assemblies of God	239
Alliance (C&MA)	32
Wesleyan	27
Southern Baptist	609
Nazarene	45
American Baptist	12
Methodist (UMC)	231
Lutheran (ELCA)	41
Presbyterian (PCUSA)	28
Episcopal	15

0% 0.5% 1.0% 1.5% 2.0%

100% of all surveyed churches are represented when all sizes are combined (0.3% have attendance of 2,000 or more)

Worship Attendance of 2,000 or More
(number and percent of each denomination's churches)

Wesleyan	12
Assemblies of God	87
Southern Baptist	179
Alliance (C&MA)	8
American Baptist	2
Methodist (UMC)	39
Nazarene	4
Lutheran (ELCA)	5
Presbyterian (PCUSA)	2
Episcopal	0

0% 0.1% 0.2% 0.3% 0.4% 0.5%

KEY

ABBREVIATION	DENOMINATION	# OF CHURCHES	YEAR OF DATA
Alliance	The Christian and Missionary Alliance	1,868	2015
American Baptist	American Baptist Churches in the U.S.A.	1,564	2014
Assemblies of God	Assemblies of God	11,941	2014
Episcopal	The Episcopal Church	6,543	2014
Lutheran	Evangelical Lutheran Church in America	9,363	2014
Methodist	United Methodist Church	31,891	2014
Nazarene	Church of the Nazarene	4,610	2015
Presbyterian	Presbyterian Church (U.S.A.)	7,271	2015
Southern Baptist	Southern Baptist Convention	39,004	2014
Wesleyan	The Wesleyan Church	1,613	2015

NOTE: The term "all churches" across these tables means all churches in this study. The percentages represent the average of all churches from the ten denominations in this study. The total of 115,873 churches in the study represent just over one-third of all U.S. Protestant churches.

Most available resources are geared, predictably, to the 85 percent of churches that have not yet broken the 200 barrier. Too often, they simply don't cover the special needs of the growing and larger church.

This chapter summarizes certain key issues necessary to break the 200 barrier. This figure is not an exact or magical number (the range is actually between 50 and 350), but it does represent a critical growth limiter that the vast majority of churches hit at one or more points in their history.

The next chapter will focus on the 400 barrier, which represents a second decisive growth point in the 350 to 600 attendance level. Chapter 12 touches on the key issues necessary to break the 800 barrier, a plateau most churches hit between 600 and 1,200.

Finally, chapter 13 discusses what may be referred to as the 10,000 down to 10 barrier. It describes how to grow bigger by becoming smaller. For that reason I entitled the chapter, "How to Break the *Care* Barrier."

Prewire the Crisis

When I checked into the hospital for surgery several years ago, the nurse stuck an intravenous needle into my arm. "What's that for?" I asked her.

"It's a precaution. If an emergency happens, we'll be ready," she said.

What a powerful analogy of how churches can better administer care in Jesus's name! We can "prewire" people so that when a crisis occurs, the church can spring into action. We can hope our people will not have to face medical tragedy, emotional grief, loneliness, conflict, or other forms of need. But since they will, why not prepare for it?

This chapter reviews how the caregiving coach style of leadership, as presented in chapters 1, 6, and 7, makes the necessary preparations to handle people's needs. As a result, the church that has put the interpersonal relationships and supportive organizational system in place before the crisis occurs is able to offer enough care that it can break one growth barrier after another.

Here, then, is a summary of what is necessary to break early growth barriers, from the 75 barrier through the 200 barrier.

First, exude a contagious desire to grow. This motivational factor makes a critical difference. If you lack a compelling vision or holy imagination for what God wants to do through you and through your church, review the implications of chapters 2 and 3.

Second, clearly articulate why, humanly speaking, your church has grown and what active ingredients need to be continued and stoked. Chapters 4 and 5 were designed to help you diagnose your church's historic track record.

Third, determine what steps are next for you to shift from solo caregiver to maker and coach of many caregivers, and vigorously pursue them. Have you analyzed your ministry style and personal behavior patterns and identified one or two specific improvements to make? How will you know, two weeks from now, whether you have grown in these areas? For guidance, review chapters 6 and 7.

Many congregations are fearful of anything—such as new people—that threatens the closeness and familiarity they currently have with one another.

Fourth, deal with institutional factors that can keep a church under 200. Why do your senior former-berries, as defined in chapter 8, not always receive newcomers with open arms? Your present membership probably has a strong desire to preserve its social intimacy. Their present size allows everyone to know, or to know about, everyone else. As a result, many congregations are fearful of anything—such as new people—that threatens the closeness and familiarity they currently have with one another.

People, including Christians, like to be comfortable. If they are convinced that growth will upset the family feeling they associate with "their" church, they may establish a surprising number of turf-protection barricades to keep new members from being absorbed.

Fifth, guard against a small-church mentality creeping back in. If you, like most ministers and lay leaders, have been shaped by a long-term pattern of small-church thinking, be prepared for the pressures that may lure you back into that paradigm. One source of these pressures will be the expectations of your church people, perhaps even of your spouse, and also your possible codependent tendency to be controlled by them. These dynamics, which range from uninformed lifelong habits to downright sabotage, received attention in chapter 8.

Another pressure to return to the old will be the disequilibrium you experience as you make the transition to a new peer group whose members are asking the same kinds of questions you are. That awkwardness was described in the section of chapter 2 on vision limiters and reintroduced at the beginning of this chapter.

Perhaps the most subtle appeal to a life of flock "petting," with its accompanying cap on growth, may come during a burst of apparently prosperous ministry. Suppose, for example, you develop your ranching skills and release a number of your people to function as lay shepherds. Suppose, further, that through the ministry of one of those whom you are discipling, a well-connected family in your community experiences a spiritual rebirth and becomes involved in your church. They, in turn, draw four other households to the church. These four newcomers likewise invite their friends, and a growth momentum is born. Your temptation, as you observe these junior newberries trying to assimilate into the existing networks and structures of the church, might be to pop on your pastor-as-the-only-shepherd cap and become the primary caregiver each time you notice a relationship gap.

Or consider the true case of a couple who provided a clear example of consummate solo caregivers. He, the only pastor of this church, could prepare an excellent sermon in ten hours a week. Then he would put in sixty additional hours of hands-on need-meeting. She, though not officially on staff, volunteered more hours than many full-time ministers put in. Their married children lived out of state, and they both seemed to have the gift of "perpetual hospitality" at their home, which adjoined the church property.

A person could walk into the church building during daylight hours, seven days a week, and anticipate being greeted by this pastor or his wife. In the evening, neither seemed too busy to take a call at home.

These wonderful Christian people went to heroic efforts to see to it that they were always available. As a result, they helped build their church to an attendance of 700. Unfortunately, however, they collapsed. He had a coronary arrest, and she became very resentful of how she felt the church had "done her husband in." They resigned and moved elsewhere, bitter and discouraged.

My point? Even if sacrificial, solo-style caregiving helps produce growth and carries you beyond the 200 barrier, you will reach a stopping point sooner or later. When you reach that capacity limit, you may well discover that your own health is in need of repair, physically, emotionally, and probably spiritually. And your church members, whom you trained to expect omnipresent hand-holding from their minister, may hound you until you or your successor resumes that level of ministry.

Finally, establish a network of lay-led small groups as the context for lay leadership development. Peter Wagner, leading pioneer authority on church growth, says, "The major difference between the church under the 200 barrier and one over the 200 barrier is fellowship groups."[9] He explains why a church must move from single cells to multiple cells if it is to grow beyond 200:

> The group dynamic theory that underlies this is the rule of 40. Forty people is the ideal size for everyone to maintain face-to-face relationship with everyone else. In a church setting the group can expand to

80 and sustain most of the interpersonal qualities. However, when it goes past 80 toward 200, the relationships are increasingly strained. By the time it gets to 150 most groups are so stressed out that they can no longer handle the thought of strangers entering the group and thereby increasing the stress. Without knowing they are doing it or without even wanting to, they relate to strangers like two identical poles of magnets.[10]

As veteran church observer Elmer Towns confirms, the wave of the future is in body life through cell groups. "To be a whole church, it must have the *cell* as well as the *celebration*,"[11] he says. He finds this model to be eminently biblical:

> The large group in the Jerusalem church met for celebration, preaching, motivation and testimony (see Acts 3:11); and in small cells for fellowship, accountability, instruction and identity (see Acts 5:42). From these observations, I conclude that the norm for the New Testament church included both small cell groups and larger celebration groups.[12]

Imagine the potential as increasing numbers of laypeople are released to be coministers of care and nurture. Meeting in groups of approximately ten people—the time-tested, scientifically validated size that allows for optimal communication—warehouses of underutilized Christians will prompt each other to love and good works.[13]

Their challenge and ongoing encouragement will come from peers who know one another's spiritual gifts and who care enough that they will not allow a friend to settle into "spectatorism." Because of the intimate, accountability-inviting context of an affinity-based group, participants will readily accept the call of God that accompanies the discovery of their gifts. The immediacy of the evangelism and discipleship that occurs in the lives of fellow cell members cannot help but shatter passivity. (Chapter 13 will present more insight into a systemic approach to lay-led small groups.)

For now, let me pose a question: If each of the world's largest churches (fellowships of 30,000 or more are found on every continent) has found that a cell system is vital to its health and ongoing growth, then what is the implication for the vitality of *your* church as a potential church of 300, 3,000 or 30,000?

My conclusion is this: sooner or later, a constantly rekindled vision of open cells led by prayerful people replicating themselves through apprentice leaders is going to produce life-changing results—two to four converts per year per group. As staff members place priority on the cultivation of the lay leadership necessary to make this happen, the dynamics of cell fertility will inevitably take over and much fruit will be harvested, including that of numerical church growth.

The implication? Make sure your people are lodged in a cell system where a lay pastoral team receives ongoing supervision and coaching from the professional staff of the church. See to it that the pastoral staff is infected with a vision so radical that it is tantamount, for many, to a change in profession: getting out of the ministry business and into a new assignment of making ministers.

> *Sooner or later, a constantly rekindled vision of open cells led by prayerful people replicating themselves through apprentice leaders is going to produce life-changing results.*

Which 200 Barrier?

Any discussion of breaking the 200 barrier raises the question of "which 200?" Is the church passing an attendance level of 200 for the first time under a founding pastor? Or maybe the church has been hovering at a 200 attendance plateau under succession of pastorates? Or perhaps the church was once very large and attendance is currently passing 200 as another stage in a journey that might end in downward demise? Each of these situations has its own uniqueness, requiring a variation in strategy.

The first of these options—the new 200—requires a high-touch environment. This stage in the congregation is heavily about community building. Often it's a new church with new growth, including a sense of excitement and momentum. At the same time, it's socially fragile because the congregation has few habits and patterns, amplified by the likelihood that churches like this tend not to have their own facilities or other ready "anchor" points.

In such high-touch situations, the pastor can be a member of a small group, providing a personal touch and modeling care until the group members become enmeshed with each other and the apprentice leader has also gelled with the group. When the powerful social binding of "belonging" takes root as people in the group begin to do life together, then the pastor moves on to a new group and repeats the cycle, again with another apprentice.

This "new 200" situation requires extra effort to keep enthusiasm high in order for the congregation to adhere to itself. Underneath that must be a strong value of doing all ministry through teams, with the emerging staff—typically volunteers and part-timers—likewise being team developers. Even a growth stage like going to two or three services needs to happen from a community-building perspective: Are we developing enough group and team leaders (of greeters, musicians, nursery care, and so forth) to staff the needed roles for the new service?

This is an excellent stage to also consider team appointments. Could you ask one group to accept responsibility as the setup/teardown team for even months (and another for the odd months)? Likewise with a quarterly rotation by other groups to handle the coffee table or be the first-impression team. Ideally, a team will agree to handle some aspect of the task for a month plus one week into the next month—the final week to serve as overlap and training for the next team.

The next two options—the plateau at 200 and the stage of decline passing through 200—involve an additional set of players: stakeholders that might invest considerable energy into preventing growth because it is likely to take away their station, as they must share their place with the new people who will show up. While the leadership team gives attention to bringing on board a new set of nesting-stage families and college-age students, they must also serve as brokers between unhappy or even recalcitrant stakeholders.

The sharing of space and stories between longtimers and newcomers happens, but with each group running on a parallel track. Each needs a proportional amount of attention from the pastor as the berry bucket metaphor of chapter 8 illustrates. Both longtimers and newcomers can receive pastoral care and meaningful connection through the class, team, and group life of the church.

One track is for the pastoral team to collaborate with stakeholders as much as possible in facilitating and supporting their existing ministries for mutual self-care. Some will be open to people who are new to the church, but it rarely works to try to plug new people into old, long-established groups. A few such groups or ministries will even close their doors. The key is for stakeholders to feel you understand and support their social situation.

The other track in turnaround situations like this—plus the "new 200" church—is for the pastoral team to give attention to cultivating new growth: making worship energetic and culturally relevant, building momentum by cheering success, establishing presence via social media, and developing groups (through new leaders) that will reach out and connect with those who are not yet part of the church community. They also work on seasonal opportunities such as Easter, Mother's Day, Thanksgiving, and Christmas as big open-door events. A third new-growth component is to serve the church's target area with appropriate charitable and good works: taking care of widows, partnering to rehab dilapidated public school classrooms, and so forth. By definition a church of 200 is a neighborhood church, not a regional church, affording constant opportunity for continual touches through community-based neighborhood engagement projects. The surrounding community needs to know: the people of this church are here to help us.

The third group—the one passing 200 as another stage in a journey that might end in downward demise—is especially likely to have a low corporate self-esteem. They may live in oversized facilities, and just keeping the roof dry is almost overwhelming. They tend to be hermit-crab churches, internally focused, consumed by maintenance, and embarrassed by what little they can do with their oversized facilities. Often this is not just an issue of an aging congregation and facility but also of a changed neighborhood situation. Some can imagine no hope for connecting with the new ethnic or racial character of the neighborhood. Others are in gentrified areas where the new levels of education in the neighborhood seem an impossible match for the present makeup of the congregation. This might require bold steps like a healthy merger (as in Warren Bird's coauthored book *Better Together*), new senior leadership, and/or other dramatic social transitions such as through the sponsoring denomination. Such declines are often irreversible without a connection to a new set of family units from the area who are able to socially integrate.

In all three approaches, the overriding strategy is for leaders to deal with people one-on-one until they can plug them into a group or ministry, anchoring them in new relationships in a social setting designed for mutual self-care.

All three groups must find ways to achieve momentum. The challenge in the "new 200" barrier is too little cohesiveness among their new adherents. The challenge with the "plateaued at 200" barrier is too much cohesiveness among their established people, which makes it hard for newcomers to adhere.

In all three approaches, the overriding strategy is for leaders to deal with people one-on-one until they can plug them into a group or ministry, anchoring them in new relationships in a social setting designed for mutual self-care. (I unpack this approach more in my book *Nine Keys to Effective Small Group Leadership: How Lay Leaders Can Establish Dynamic and Healthy Cells, Classes and Teams.*)

Imagine a war situation in which a soldier limps back into camp and the first person to meet him is the general. This officer compassionately pats the soldier on the back with an expression of appreciation, but promptly says, "Soldier, what is your unit?" and then points him there. The general has a notion that other people are already present who are far better equipped to handle this soldier. Can you build that kind of care-ready environment in your church?

Properties and Facilities

As a church grows toward and beyond the 200 barrier, the leadership frequently faces new questions about building programs, facility enlargements, and property acquisitions. Here are the questions I am asked most frequently. (I will deal with multiple worship services in chapter 12.)

1. Our people are talking about enlarging our facility to reduce overcrowding. How do I know if that is the solution needed?

Your most crucial capacity determiner stems from your parking availability, not your seating capacity (see example in Figure 7). In growing churches, lack of onsite parking often creates tension for both members and visitors. The rare exceptions are those located adjacent to public parking areas or to curbside parking on sidewalk-lined streets. For urban churches, the exceptions are those located near one or more public transportation stops.

If you pastor a growing church that fills its auditorium to more than 80 percent of its capacity on average, then the overcrowdedness (over a two- to three-year period) will tend to limit the growth of your church. Exceptions occur if you are ministering in an ethnic community that is underserviced, if you have a strong cell system, and/or if your church has an exceptional platform appeal such as miracle ministries, widely known and advertised musical talent, or regionally broadcast television or radio programming.

But do not be hasty in concluding that the 80 percent fill is your problem when, in reality, the barrier may be elsewhere. Divide your average attendance by two and a half people per car. If you draw a lot of single adults, divide by one and a half people per car. Do you have enough easy-to-reach parking spots?

Figure 7

When You Expand to Multiple Services, Then Parking Typically Becomes Your Choke Point, Even More Than Seating

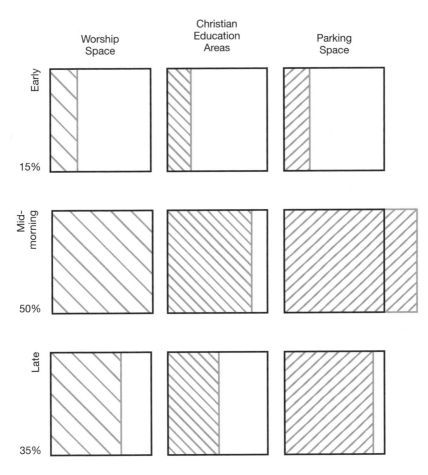

161

Even if the answer is yes, you still might not be ready for a building program. Instead, a wise next step is to consider establishing dual usage of your current facilities.

If you are short on Sunday school space, install two Sunday school sessions, one before and one after worship. If your auditorium is small, then offer two worship services with Sunday school in between. If you are tight all the way around, think about holding Sunday school and worship simultaneously. Send everybody from the first hour home (or to serve as a volunteer for the second hour) and then repeat the process for the second hour. By creatively using your existing space without enlargement, you can increase your membership by 50 percent or better.

In short, if a church is serious about growth, it will demonstrate that commitment by making an adequate amount of parking available and by maximizing the use of its physical plant. The difference between pastors who can lead their churches forward and those who cannot frequently expresses itself over this issue: whether the pastor is willing to envision new facilities, raise the necessary money, and lead the parishioners through the accompanying pains of acquisition and adjustment.

If you can lead your people to accept the idea of a different use of their time and space, then you have probably developed the trust and skill necessary to lead them to do other things they need for growth overall.

2. Our church is almost ready for a building program. Should we expand where we are or relocate?

In theory it is easier to relocate than to expand, because land can be cheaper, building from scratch is easier than remodeling, and parking can be chosen and planned. In reality, however, most churches end up enlarging in their present locations.

I recommend you plan for both, remembering all the while that most of your solutions will not come together overnight.

First, establish a "green-line district" around your present church facility. This represents properties you would like to acquire. Begin buying them. Be careful, though, not to take on more debt than you can handle.

Over ten years, you can accumulate a sizable amount of contiguous real estate. After the land has been unoccupied and off the tax rolls, your city's leaders will be likely to favor putting the land to better use.

Develop a plan for local expansion and begin securing the necessary legal permissions. You will need to build personal relationships with the homeowners near to your facility. You will probably have to outlast certain local politicians, extremist environmental groups, and others with an antidevelopment attitude. Of course, if you decide that you own more real estate than you need, or if you opt to relocate, you can usually sell.

Meanwhile, make sure you are aware of every available option. Consider church planting and multisite approaches. Have multiple worship services to maximize use of your present facilities.

If you think creatively and plan long range, you will ultimately develop the kind of campus you need.

3. Our church is looking for land. Is there an optimal ratio of acreage to congregation size?

In suburban settings, one acre can handle between 100 and 300 people, depending on your programming, how many people drive to your services, the average number of people per car, and the "green space" requirements of your local zoning board.

Do not count on a traditional program to stack people in at 300 per acre. You will need several turns of the auditorium for that: maybe a Saturday or Sunday night service, back-to-back Sunday morning services, and more home-based cell groups than on-premises Sunday school classes.

4. We're choosing between a visible site that has an inadequate roadway and a hard-to-see location with easy access. What do you recommend for our church's property search?

Accessibility is almost always more important than visibility. You may have a worship center perched on top of a hill, but if there is only one road leading up there, and it is not clearly marked, you are in trouble. The same principle holds for the church facility that is adjacent to a well-traveled highway but is really four confusing miles away from the exit ramp.

The more visible site inevitably costs more. You are better off moving in the direction of accessibility and using the dollars saved to advertise your church and its programs.

5. We haven't expanded in many years. What are some common snags to watch for when we work with architects and city councils?

Officials may not fully understand your site-load needs. City codes, for example, may permit you to build an auditorium based on five or six seats per car in your parking lot. But church trends are for fewer and fewer people per car, especially in upper middle class and suburban situations. So your architect may fix you up legally, but you will encounter the immediate problem of not being able to park everyone.

Instead, make your own site-load calculation by tallying the total number of bodies on a per-hour basis. That is, take your busiest hour—say Sunday at 11:00 a.m.—and calculate the anticipated capacity of your worship space including choir, plus your nursery, plus the number of people using your Christian education space (children and adults).

Next, figure out how many people come per car during that busiest hour. Divide that number into your per-hour total and you have a more realistic site load (review Figure 7).

Be prepared, however, for the findings from your studies to lead you to make better use of your space. You will discover, for example, that if you emphasize home groups over traditional Sunday school, you will reduce parking needs on Sundays (not to mention the larger benefit of engendering greater care). Switching your youth group to the first hour on Sundays, or using three different choirs instead of one stay-all-morning choir, may likewise realign your parking area's pressure points.

6. I'm convinced that our community views our church as too crowded for anyone new, but our board doesn't feel that way. What should I do?

Unchurched people view churches in the same way legendary baseball player Yogi Berra described an overcrowded restaurant: "Don't go there to eat; nobody goes there, because you can never find a seat." In other words, "They're so successful that it's not worth going!" It takes only two seasons to teach an entire community that you do not have room for prospective new members. Even a 5 percent turn-away factor communicates that you are too full. Then the gripe factor comes into play: a satisfied customer tells three people, but a dissatisfied customer tells seven.

What to do? First, ask yourself if you have built a climate on your church board that genuinely wants growth. Or would board members rather preserve their memory of the past and their comfort in the present? Do they see the grassy spot in front of the church building as the former swamp which they filled and cultivated or as the next site for "phase two" of the parking lot plan?

Second, probe to find out if they are aware of how visitors feel. If your old-timers arrive early enough that they can park in the best spots, do they know that the newcomers must walk across icy slush or broken pavement? In short, create a contagious vision of the harvest God wants to grant to your church.

In short, create a contagious vision of the harvest God wants to grant to your church.

7. In light of rising costs for land and buildings, we want to lease. What are the minimum facility requirements we should consider?

First, find major meeting space for worship. Often this same area can accommodate large-group fellowship occasions as well. Ideally it will also be available during the week for times of leadership training.

In addition, you will want child-care space to accompany your big meetings. It should be clean, safe, and easily accessible from your major meeting room(s).

Finally, you will need administration space for pastors and office help and storage space for church equipment and supplies.

How does this list differ from that for a church building committee? The missing ingredient is classrooms. Historically, a huge percentage of a construction budget gets sunk into facilities, such as for teaching space used only one or two days a week. Churches of the future, particularly urban churches, will be pressured by economics to make greater use of home-based or other off-premises groups.

FOR FURTHER THOUGHT

1. How comfortable are you with the assumptions outlined at the beginning of this chapter?
2. What surprised you about the growth statistics cited in this chapter? What suspicions did you already have?
3. Look over the summary of the issues necessary for breaking the 200 barrier. Which reflect a strength of your church? Which pinpoint areas in need of improvement?
4. How essential is the small group to the overall health of a church? To its numerical growth? Why?
5. What property and facilities issue is most pressing for your church? What are your top three options at present?

How to Break the 400 Barrier

As a church moves beyond the 200 barrier it encounters a fresh set of challenges. Certain issues that previously were of minor concern now take center stage. Pastors and lay leaders begin to ask new questions about church boards, staffing, and delegation of duties. These three administrative issues are pivotal if a church is to offer adequate care to hundreds of active participants.

What answers will your church give to the crucial questions this challenge raises? Your response will have a major influence on how quickly and painlessly you are able to break the 400 barrier—which may occur at 300, 400, 500, or even 600. The exact pinch point is not a specific number but the point where your structure must change to include additional layer(s) of spiritual caregivers and minister makers.

This chapter will not tell you where to find enough new people so that your attendance can reach 400. It assumes that your current congregation has an adequate contact base to reach far more than 400 newcomers. Rather, this chapter describes how to prepare for, lead, and care for additional growth.

How Best to Work with Your Board

At the smaller stage, the patriarchs, matriarchs, and heavy donors run the church, whether or not they are on the board. The real votes almost never take place in the board meetings. Instead, the decisions that determine whether the big donors and people of influence will back something are made in living rooms, on the phone, via texting, or over coffee. The board simply plays catch-up with what has been decided. The real power is based in an informal group, not in the pastor or board.

As a church moves beyond the 200 level, it will need to develop a way of leading and governing that goes beyond the energy and personal availability of its pastor. An expansion of the paid staff must occur, usually in a somewhat predictable order: administrative assistant(s), a custodian, a worship leader, a youth leader, a children's ministry leader, an office manager, and a financial secretary or bookkeeper. These positions are often part-time at first, moving to full-time as finances allow. Board members will be added and will tend to be assigned to encourage the ministry areas led by the expanding staff. Board meetings discuss actual ministry programs. I will offer more details about these positions later in this chapter.

Later, when a congregation begins to envision itself capable of going beyond 800, it must make certain organizational shifts to continue in the growth process. One of the most important issues at that point will be to negotiate the changing role of the church governing board. Planning and administration must become a staff function and not a board responsibility. Beyond 400, church boards take on increased importance and influence. When a church reaches an average attendance of 400 or so, generally the members of the board are the people who *can* make a difference or are the *spouses* of the people who can make a difference. The formal and informal power structures have come together. These boards can actually accomplish something. Such boards in the 400–800 church function as management or operating committees, with volunteer (unpaid) members who donate time and talents to governance. This arrangement is so successful and widespread that most congregations never go beyond a board-governed structure. Founder pastors who lead a church from new or small to beyond 1,000 frequently struggle with the eventual transition from board-led to staff-led organizations. (I will say more about this in a following chapter.)

As a church increases in size to beyond 800 or 1,000, the oligarchy of power tends to shift to be centered in the one or two closest friends of the senior pastor (or of the senior pastor's spouse), plus the pastor's closest aides on the staff. This group, typically fewer than a dozen people, comes to exercise most of the control over the church.

If such a coterie is right with God, orthodox in doctrine, and balanced in its view of the church's mission, the church will accomplish great things. The board at this level appears to mostly document and approve what has already been decided in planning sessions among staff.

Boards Are Essential

Beyond 400, boards are helpful, even essential. The pastor who tries to lead a church without a board or to play games with it will soon encounter great trouble. The households represented on the board are typically those of the primary donors, the primary influencers, the primary recruiters of volunteer energies, and even the primary conduits for reaching large segments of unchurched people.

The need for shared vision and camaraderie at the board level is so critical that it cannot be left to chance. An enthusiastic "Glad to see you! How've you been doing?" makes a huge difference in building an esprit de corps, as do pats on the back, good-natured ribbing, and other gestures of personal concern.

As the church enlarges beyond 400, it becomes crucial to identify what programs will be organized and supported with budgets and

> *The staff will provide direction, the board will provide policy, and everyone else— 95 percent or more of the church—will be involved in hands-on ministry.*

staff and board oversight. For many leaders, this is an ideal church size, where non-clergy members have significant roles in governance and ministry. As the attendance exceeds 800, additional shifts must occur to prepare for continued growth.

At a larger future state, the team that must drive the program, provide the vision, do the planning, and create the budgets is the church staff, not the board. The term *staff* refers to people in management roles in a church's organization, regardless of whether they are paid or volunteer, ordained or lay, full-time or part-time, as long as they meet this qualification: they have agreed to take assignments from the senior leadership and be held accountable.

This staff then goes to the board mainly for approvals and policy. The board, as well as the other people of influence, comes to understand that the staff will provide direction, the board will provide policy, and everyone else—95 percent or more of the church—will be involved in hands-on ministry.

Dangers of a Small-Church Mentality

Many pastors and board members cut their ecclesiastical eyeteeth in a small church. Some may have gained experience in a midsize church, but it probably behaved like a small church. In either of those contexts the boards typically hire staff to do the ministry.

So, when the church is midsize, board members see themselves as the structurally empowered leaders of the church. They want to set the budget, the plan, and the dream. Then they want their paid, professional clergy to carry it out.

In other words, board members designate themselves as the managers and the church staff as the ministers (see Figure 8). That leaves the majority of the church in a spectator's inactive role at worst, and a semipassive dependency at best. This pattern helps explain why so many North American churches do not grow (a perspective I will expand in chapter 13).

If a church is to become bigger, the staff must commission ministry while taking policy direction from boards. That represents a world of difference from the typical small-church arrangement. This new set of roles requires an important transfer in the focus of initiative-taking. Staff members pick up management responsibilities and do whatever direct primary-care shepherding they can as they are training laypeople for such ministry.

This new assignment causes dismay for many staff people, who may feel the loss of direct caring ministry so deeply that they seek out a smaller church or a church with a smaller vision that will allow them a continued shepherding role. Alternately, many such staff people are too dependent on strokes from others to give place to developing lay leaders who are willing to accept accountability and responsibility for caring ministry. As a consequence, those underutilized lay servants bail out and go to places where they are allowed to minister.

Figure 8

In Many Churches, Pastors
Are the Paid Caregivers

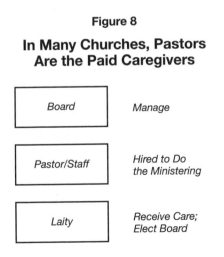

Board	Manage
Pastor/Staff	Hired to Do the Ministering
Laity	Receive Care; Elect Board

Resistance to New Board Roles

Growing churches that thrive at the midsize level can so enjoy their experiences that they are reluctant to imagine what changes will be required of them as they grow beyond 800. Lay leaders may buck the change from setting the church's course to being a policy-making board. Certain laypersons derive a feeling of power from being able to say, "No, no, no" at the board level. Clergy staff persons who previously allowed those powerful people to stay on the board while they themselves did the ministry must break two patterns: their own and that of their board.

If lay resistance surfaces during this transition, the reason often is that the "old guard" fear that if they cannot influence who leads the church, then they will lose control of "their" church. They lose sight of the harvest to which the church is called and instead focus on their experience within the comfort zone of the congregation.

This diagnosis, which was analyzed in the berry bucket section of chapter 8, is absolutely right. To grow beyond an attendance of 800 to 1,200, a church must have staff-initiated leadership.

The long process of making this shift, both in attitude and administrative structure, can begin when a church is crossing the 400 mark. It can begin to operate in such a way that the staff is not driven by a volunteer-controlled board.

Why? At some point the church will have become so big that it is no longer practical for its volunteer board members, who are in effect part-timers, to manage the church's coordination tasks. Too many details arise that cannot wait until the board convenes each month. No matter how efficient the board tries to be, it can regularly bottleneck the staff's efforts to build growth momentum.

Streamlined Church Boards

An increasing number of churches, however, realize that the harvest potential at their doorsteps is enormous. They want to be available to

God for whatever doors the Holy Spirit might open. They are willing to be stretched into new roles that will allow for greater growth.

For such churches, what should be the continuing role of an executive board or governing committee? (See Figure 9.)

An increasing number of churches are willing to be stretched into new roles that will allow for greater growth.

1. Authorize policy.

Policy establishes the basis for standard operating procedures. It helps both pastor and people evaluate whether they are on track in what they are trying to do. It establishes precedents for operating in a rational and predictable way. It ensures that a church's values are contained in church-planning statements.

Policy, for example, says: "Before we purchase this real estate, the following checks will have taken place." Policy may also be general. "We will have a written annual plan; we will have a financial audit conducted by an outside accountant; the senior minister, with the appropriate executive staff, will recommend the hiring and firing of all staff, and will inform the board of such actions."

The smaller the church, the more the policy is shaped by the personalities of the people it will affect. The larger the church, the more policy is shaped by the issues involved. For example, the launching of a support-and-recovery ministry might receive impetus in a smaller church from a board member concerned about her wayward son. In the larger church the launching of a new ministry might be guided more by overall plans, objectives, and demographic issues.

Some churches become wrapped up in policy for the wrong reasons. For example, consider what happens when the pastor or leader is lacking in confrontational skills. I knew of one minister who spent three years guiding his board to rewrite the church constitution because he could not deal with one difficult elder. You cannot develop effective policy without first having appropriate people skills.

173

What are the advantages of having a board that authorizes policy? First, it creates a forum for well-placed members to monitor quality-of-ministry issues. They have ears to the ground and can advise the senior leadership on the spiritual health and operational flow of the church.

Second, board members serve as role models. By showing other parishioners what it means to be exemplary lay leaders, they help preserve values that the pastors are building into the church.

Third, this kind of board marks the difference between the senior leadership's thinking out loud and the resulting formalized, approved, officially sanctioned plans. In this way the board's formal role solidifies the planning process.

Finally, the board contributes to a unified vision. If, for example, the senior pastor has difficulty with some aspect of staff management, the board can affirm, "We agree with you; take it back and tell the staff to shape it up this way." The staff writes the plan, the board approves it, and the leader guides its formation and approval.

Figure 9

Boards of Lay Leaders Are Most Effective as Quasi-Staff at Churches in the 400–800 Range

1. Nominations	4. Budget
2. Personnel	5. Policies
3. Plans	6. Mission

Governing Board as Management Committee

2. Nominate.

A board is necessary to designate who does what in the church, especially who sits on key boards, teams, and committees. The two groups on the board most critical for steering the direction of the church are typically the nominating team and the parish-relations team.

Whenever possible, therefore, the pastor (or a close and loyal friend) should be on these boards. The pastor who seems indifferent to who is part of the nomination process either has no plans to lead the church to grow, is incredibly naive, or has a spouse who is well connected politically and in every other sense to the congregation. (This spousal factor cannot be overrated.)

The future tells us that appointment, rather than election, will be the more common way people come to ministry. A church that hands most of its ministry slots to elected positions is on a collision course. Elections too often operate based on popularity, not ministry competency.

3. Oversee senior staff succession.

When a senior pastor retires, falls, moves, or dies, the board triggers all the mechanisms necessary to secure a replacement. Sometimes the board helps the senior pastor fill other key staff positions. Otherwise, the board should not be very concerned with the hiring and firing of staff. As much as possible, the senior staff will decide staffing issues.

4. Resolve staff conflicts.

Church boards spend a lot of time, both in and out of the boardroom, reducing the level of staff infighting.

What causes such widespread staff conflict? Most pastoral staff enter their first multistaff roles with the expectation that they will have no boss. Any attempt to impose "boss-ship" usually results in all kinds of dirty fighting.

In dysfunctional families (which, unfortunately, describes the families of many clergy in North America[1]) even spiritual people behave carnally when they face conflict. To make matters worse, the passive-aggressive personality is probably the character trait most often selected for ministry. The candidate is passive enough for others to think he or she is controllable or innocuous. But the aggressive side of his or her character knows how to be angry, deal spitefully, and keep a frustrated or depressive spouse in a state of codependency.[2]

If senior pastors do not know when to fire people, and if their staff consistently manifest poor communication skills, the resulting multistaff melee will be a killing ground with a constant undercurrent of conflict. This is where boards have to step in.

5. Implement mission and plans.

If a church has a mission statement and direction, boards will want to be part of an active planning process. They prefer that the staff not do it all themselves; they want a sense of ownership. The key is to direct the board's energy and skill into owning and fleshing out the pastor's vision, not wading through the details of implementation.

> Mission comes from prayer, from the written Word of God, and from discussion with God's people.

As deep and wide as the senior pastor's vision is, so goes the organization. If the senior pastor (or senior team), like Moses, spends time with God on the mountain, the plans that come to the church board will be durable. Mission comes from prayer, from the written Word of God, and from discussion with God's people.

Ultimately, all church mission statements have certain common threads. They contain a vertical dimension, such as loving and obeying God, and they emphasize a horizontal dimension: how Christians treat those both inside and outside the church. They answer the question of why God left the church here on earth.

The secret of success is not the wording but the fact that the people on the board have dug the mission statement out of the Bible for themselves, have decided to commit their church to it, and have made it theirs.

6. Approve budgets.

Many churches accomplish their planning through a budgeting process. They have not realized that they can create a plan and then match dollars to it. As Lyle Schaller points out, the typical atmosphere in a nongrowing church is a fight over how to split the pie and divide the anticipated spoils. The common scenario is that the board says no to every opportunity that presents itself and thus the church never has the funds to do the innovative things that are needed.

According to Schaller, the most important shift a board can make is toward an opportunity focus. Lead your board to consider what needs to be done and what God will bless. Then build your budget from that point.[3]

A leader has no power in an organization until he or she can influence a group to say yes. In a church, as in any bureaucracy, virtually no one has the power to say yes. A church board tends to accumulate conservators, thereby gathering in one room the biggest group of potential blockers in the church. What a wonderful opportunity for the pastor to help them turn loose of their precious treasure and commit themselves to faith!

Board members often will permit their pastors to take leadership in direct proportion to the pastor's willingness to raise money. And to whatever extent the pastor develops a track record for gathering funds, the board will give him or her freedom to direct the spending of it.

After two to three years of solid financial leadership, the senior pastor can then ask for expenditures without the board becoming uptight. By contrast, when the board has to bail out the pastor's financial decisions, they are very reluctant to grant permission for their leadership to spend more.

This principle holds true in other areas. Do you want to have power to guide your staff? Deal with your own dirty laundry. Handle discipline and conflict within your staff. Show skill in how you dismiss poorly performing staff members, or, more likely, in how you learn to do a better job of supervising them.

What about staff compensation? This issue will probably remain a board decision, but as your church becomes larger, your budget will tend to have a one-line total that reads "salaries," and the breakdown will be created by a personnel team.[4]

7. Be a safety valve.

A board enhances two-way interpretation of program purposes and effects. When people want to complain about how something was handled, the board can say, "No, we talked about that, and here's what we found."

8. Participate in a growth regimen.

Laypeople on the main church board will receive special attention from the pastor who promotes their own personal spiritual growth.

Pastors are forever having to ask themselves, *How should I spend my time?* The most strategic answer is to work with leaders, such as your staff and your board. Give them some quality time. They should expect that you will not leave them in the same spiritual condition as when they first came on the board.

How the Management Staff Responds

When board and committee roles have been clarified, the net result is more executive responsibility for the professional staff. Their role is now to utilize managerial skills for planning, communicating, problem identification, and problem solving. They also must expand their personnel skills in areas of staff selection, assignment, and team building.

What does this look like? First, the senior pastor becomes the primary person who articulates and communicates the vision and accepts responsibility for the oversight of the staff (see Figure 10). This directional leader paints the picture of the preferred future: what must be done in the long view for effective ministry, soliciting the church's commitment to that ideal. This is not done by edict or coercion; rather, vision persuades. The pastor creates an enthusiastic and dedicated commitment to a goal because it is right for the times, right for the organization, and right for the people who are part of the church.

For example, the world's largest church, Yoido Full Gospel Church, founded by David Yonggi Cho in Seoul, Korea, did not develop 55,000 cell-group leaders by accident. They existed, by the grace of God, because the founding pastor had a vision of what would happen if he would release and support laypeople to care for one another. He realized that for this to happen he would need to provide them with tools and supervision. So he envisioned one staff member for every fifty cells, and that is exactly what God helped him put in place over time.

Second, the staff members accept roles as being part of a management committee and as overseers of the ministry. They interpret the senior pastor's vision into the how-tos and time frames. The staff, then, must be skilled in leadership development, administration, and delegation.

Third, the church board becomes smaller—ideally a single-digit size including one senior pastor plus a handful of administratively gifted laypeople.

Staffing: First Things First

Is there a preferred sequence for adding staff to a growing church? Can certain tools (such as those highlighted in chapter 3, note 10) predict how well a prospective staff member would mesh with the rest of the team?

Yes. Before trying to use those tools, however, the senior pastor must understand a certain role change is necessary to be an effective leader of staff: from being a manager to being a leader. What is the difference? Leaders set a direction; managers outline the steps to the destination.

Figure 10

Board Members Need to Learn
When to Wear Which Hat

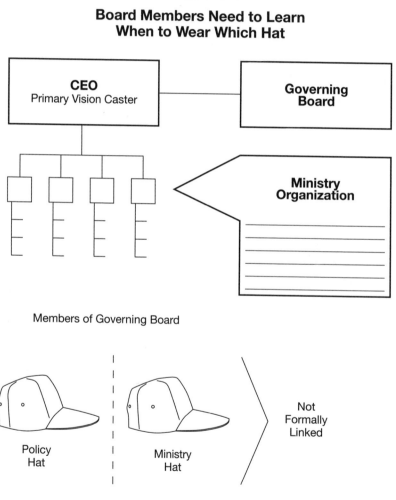

180

Many of you will have to do both jobs to some extent. But most churches (and businesses) are overmanaged and underled. Pastors are more obsessed with doing things *right* than with doing the right *things*. They give more attention to efficiency than to effectiveness.

A leader gives direction by calling for a vision to come into reality. A manager sees to it that the vision gets accomplished through others. "This is the way to the promised land, and the journey starts right over there," says the leader. Everything else can be done by someone else.

The first step in bringing on new staff is to determine how you will disengage this person in the event the arrangement goes awry. My observation has been that a large-church pastor's first few experiences in hiring lead to a lot of bruising. Sadly, too many cope with the pain by resolving not to hire anyone again. But eventually they acknowledge they must develop or bring on more staff.

Most churches are overmanaged and underled.

The pathway forward for pastors learning how to work in a multi-staff situation is identifying the root problem, which often stems from the assignment-and-evaluation process being mucky. If no clear expectations have been set, the level of accountability cannot be focused.

The next step is to select the best candidate. That means taking the time to evaluate at least three nominees. The cost of the interviewing process and of checking multiple references on each person is small compared with the damage, legal and otherwise, that could result if you bring on the wrong person and do not handle their termination swiftly and decently.

Then prepare a description including specific outcomes of what you want this next staff member to do. Remember, though, that you will have a harder time getting work out of people than hiring them. While most pastors profit from having clerical or administrative assistance, the tendency is to hire a trained, program-staff caliber person and then offer the newcomer no greater opportunity than that of being a sidekick.

Instead, pinpoint the results you want and determine your staff needs accordingly. My recommendation is that you hire leaders to produce new lay leaders. If staff members are not in the business of grooming leaders, then you cannot afford to hire them. A new staff member ought to be able to produce fifty new lay leaders (people who lead others) within a three-year period.

Staffing Trends for Today

With this perspective in mind, you are ready to ask what specific roles you want new staff members to fill. The most common pattern today is to start with a senior minister and a part-time administrative assistant. As a church consistently passes 100 in regular attendance, the office manager works full-time and many volunteers are heading up various ministries.

By the time a church bumps against an attendance of 200, it will have started to add a part-time minister of youth, a part-time minister of music, and perhaps a part-time custodian. It will continue to have many volunteer ministry leaders.

As this common progression continues to 300, the youth minister works full-time and an extra part-time administrative assistant has come on board, perhaps in a specialty role like bookkeeper. Interns may become involved at this point. By 400 the music staff either works full-time or adds part-time assistants, the second administrative assistant works full-time, and the church might add another part-time custodian, depending on its facility needs.

By 500, a church will have added some specialty associate ministers in various life-stage divisions, such as children, collegians, young adults, or senior adults. As the growth continues, a full-time business manager will be brought on staff.[5]

The percentage of part-time staff has increased in recent years. So has outsourced staff such as payroll, graphic design, custodial, and so forth. Administrative assistants are fewer in number as the growth of technology has led staff to increasingly manage their own communication. The staff-to-attender ratio in larger churches now averages 1:76, according to Leadership Network research (combining part-timers into full-time equivalents).[6]

Is this overall pattern the best way to go? While it contains much wisdom, one flaw cannot be overlooked: it tends to separate the senior minister from the lay-ministry organization of the church. That broken connection is one of the things that accounts for poor performance in many of the churches I have studied.

In other words, when the senior pastor is not in direct contact with volunteer leaders—the media team, the choir directors, Sunday school teachers, welcome team leaders, head deacons, youth program people—there tends to be a deficiency of supervision or vision from the senior pastor. Staff, in their middleman's role between senior leadership and lay leaders, tend to insulate the senior pastor's vision rather than translate it.

This dilemma raises a question of delegation: Is vision something that should be left to the staff, or can it effectively be transmitted through the ranks? Increasingly my research shows that organizational hierarchies are being compressed and leaders are finding great benefit from having direct contact with their crew chiefs.[7]

How to Improve Your Delegation Skills

One of the keys to effective leadership is to work from your areas of strength, not weakness. As Peter Drucker, a leading writer in management science, has said, the purpose of organization is to make weakness irrelevant.[8] To maximize what you do best, you need to be effective in empowering others.

Is the purpose of delegation, then, to get rid of work you do not want to do? Absolutely not. If your primary motive is to develop people, and to develop leaders in particular, then the art of delegation can become a powerful tool in the discipleship process.

To maximize what you do best, you need to be effective in empowering others.

To do that you must gain a clear understanding of an important issue: levels of authority. That is, when you decide to delegate something, you need to specify what kind of permission and accountability is expected.

How do you decide what level of delegation is appropriate? Ask yourself: *What is the importance of the task I am delegating and to whom am I giving the assignment?* The more mature the person, the deeper level you can assign. Also, you might have a highly trusted person but not fully relinquish the responsibility.

How do you determine the layering of authority? The layers posited in literature on management range from three levels to eight.[9] I prefer these six levels, which move from shallow to deep:

1. Give me a report on the problem and I'll take action.
2. Study the problem and make a recommendation.
3. Analyze the situation, propose a course of action that you will take, but wait for my approval.
4. Analyze the situation, describe your proposed plan of action, and follow through unless I say no.
5. Take action and tell me what you did.
6. Take care of the situation. No need to report back to me.

Our findings are that most leaders and managers know far more about delegating than they act on. Why? As the following self-evaluation moment may well confirm, and the shift from solo caregiver to maker of other caregivers theme of this book explains, church leaders have a strong drive to do everything themselves.

SELF-EVALUATION MOMENT

How well do you delegate? Take this brief quiz and find out.

Yes/No

_____ 1. Are you afraid your people will make mistakes?

_____ 2. Do you frequently take work home or work late at the office?

_____ 3. Does your operation function smoothly when you're absent?

_____ 4. Do you spend more time working on details than you do on planning and supervising?

_____ 5. Is your follow-up procedure adequate?

_____ 6. Do you regularly overrule or reverse decisions made by those on your team?

_____ 7. Do you bypass others by making decisions that are part of their jobs?

_____ 8. Do you do several things your assistants could, and should, be doing?

_____ 9. If you were incapacitated for six months, is there someone who could readily take your place?

_____10. Will there be a big pile of paper requiring your action when you return from a trip or absence?

To score yourself, add one point for each "yes" answer to numbers 3, 5, and 9, and one point for each "no" answer to numbers 1, 2, 4, 6, 7, 8, and 10. A good score is 8 or above.[10] A score of 5 or below is the normal range for ministers I interview.

The pastor or lay leader who is a caregiving coach understands that some people are empowered by group discussion and specific commissioning while others are empowered by a simple "Go for it." Your recognition of the difference between the independent initiative takers and committee-empowered parishioners helps you to make appropriate assignments.

Where do you begin? Review your activities of the last week. What percent were ones that only you could do and only you should do?

Next, make a list of all the church responsibilities you have already delegated to other staff members, clerical assistants, volunteer workers, and any others. What additional obligations could you delegate? Which activities are you uncertain about delegating? What activities are you doing that no one, including yourself, should do?

Finally, work through the following self-evaluation moment to pinpoint the delegation-related reasons preventing you from being a more effective rancher.

What does this process look like as you identify and coach current lay shepherds to become "ranchers" by developing more shepherds? Emerging caregivers are not always apparent to pastors and leaders. Their talents and gifts may go unrecognized because of a lack of focus to discern their presence. In such cases, coaching consists of reviewing, on an individual basis, each person in the care of the care provider, discerning the gifts and talents of each person, and praying for their discernment and development. In our overly busy world, haste and preoccupation may blind us to potential even in those close to us.

Another reason emerging leaders are not recognized is they may present themselves uncomfortably, as a challenge to leaders. What appears to a leader as rebellion and disruption may actually be a misreading of an emergent leader spontaneously acting out their call but without permission. Coaching in such cases involves a reframing of the rising leader's behaviors.

SELF-EVALUATION MOMENT

What are your greatest obstacles to becoming a coach and maker of other caregivers? Circle the two most important.

1. I don't know how; I was never trained in supervising others.

2. I'm fighting a long-standing habit of doing everything myself.

3. My church doesn't expect me to be a "rancher" or delegator.

4. Frankly, I receive too much ego satisfaction from being needed.

5. I'm not a ministry coach because the job of training laypeople is too hard.

6. I'm not a ministry coach because I feel my laypeople are inadequate.

7. I'm not a ministry coach because my laypeople feel inadequate.

8. I'm unable to find willing workers to whom I can delegate.

9. I'm too insecure to shift from pastor as primary caregiver to pastor as coach and maker of other caregivers.

10. I don't see ministry coaching as what I'm supposed to do.

What will be your next step in overcoming this barrier?

If you do not delegate and empower others effectively, your church's growth will eventually stop. Your fatigue can lead to decisions of such poor quality that you may sabotage yourself.

How, then, do you stay rested? Stop doing things that other people could do. Focus your energies on those things that only you can do. Pass the rest of the work to your team. Keep growing in this all-important area.

SELF-EVALUATION MOMENT

Each of the following examples, if not handled correctly, could result in an assignment that boomerangs back to the one who delegated it. In each, if you were the pastor, what could you do to make sure the original assignments remained delegated?

1. "We've been having trouble with the heating unit in the family life center," says one of the trustees to a staff pastor. "I think it needs to be replaced. But before I authorize the expenditure, would you mind having it evaluated?"

2. "I know you don't have time to deal with it now," says the children's director to the minister of education, "but we have a major space-usage

conflict between the Sunday school and the Pioneer Girls club. Could you give it some thought and get back to me?"

3. "Pastor," reads a note from the music director that was left on the pastor's desk during the lunch hour, "please review the enclosed plans for an Easter pageant we'd like to create. I would like to commission the program at our planning committee, which meets tonight. Please get back to me before then."

4. "Pastor," says the Sunday school superintendent for the junior-high boys' program, "we keep losing leaders. If we don't get some help soon, we're going to lose our remaining teachers. I'm out of ideas, so I figured it is your turn now."[11]

Solutions: Set a date with the person to work on the problem together. Decline the request by putting the ball back in the staff person's court. Do not allow staff to give you deadlines without first giving a verbal okay. Clarify lines of responsibility so that each person knows his or her role.

The Challenge before You

Breaking the 400 barrier may not be for every person or every church. But chances are that many God-gifted people in your church have not yet reached their potential. As a result, a ripened harvest awaits capable leaders who mobilize their laypeople to "go and make disciples of all nations" (Matt. 28:19).

Nothing can substitute for enjoying God for who He is and taking time to smell life's roses. The management insights of this chapter are not intended to suck you into a bottomless vortex of greater activity.

But perhaps God also wants to be a greater part of your ministry and life than He is now. Perhaps God has a greater future for you than you have even begun to imagine. Will you purpose before Him to be all that He calls you to become?

FOR FURTHER THOUGHT

1. How does the development of your own church board compare with the pattern described in this chapter? Where are you now? In what ways are you moving or not moving toward the next phase?

2. How distinct and identifiable in your church are the roles of: (1) the chief executive officer and staff, (2) the board, and (3) the ministry leaders? How would your key board members answer that question?

3. If the senior pastor asked you to reshape the function of your church board so that it matched the description found in this chapter, what "hoops" would you need to go through? Which step of the process would be the most sensitive?

4. When your church hired its most recent staff person, by what criteria did you decide on the responsibilities of that person? On the personality strengths needed by that person?

5. What are your strongest skills in delegating? Your greatest areas for improvement? What was the most recent major project you delegated? Did you assign a specific level of authority? What is a recent project that you could have delegated but did not? Why did you not delegate it?

How to Break the 800 Barrier

The greatest challenge facing most North American churches is to break the 200 barrier. The few who breach that attendance level and continue to grow through 400 then face another critical growth point somewhere between the 600 and 1,200 size.

To cross that hurdle, a church's leaders must continue to hone their leader-making empowerment abilities. Otherwise problems of ministry will cause too much fatigue and inadequate spans of care will surface. I address both these issues below, because they try to creep in the window of a pastor's office no matter how large the church becomes.

In general, however, skill sharpening is more the need of leadership who are trying to move from the 200 barrier to the 800 barrier. A church wanting to increase beyond the 800 barrier must address something greater than proficiency training; it must introduce certain fundamental, significant changes in the church's organizational structure.

One of those changes, the shifting role of the church board, received attention in chapter 11. By the time a church reaches the 800 barrier, the transfer of initiative-taking must have left the purview of the board and been reseated as the domain of the senior staff.

Other necessary changes deal with marketing, facilities usage, and organizational design. This chapter will address each of those issues. First, however, we need to review the principle of multiplying leaders for caring ministry.

Solve Your Fatigue Problems

What motivates a pastor serving a multistaff church, which ministers to hundreds of people weekly, to come to a seminar entitled "Beyond 800"? Of the more than two thousand ministers who have gone through this conference, which I taught for many years, a sizable number had reached a threshold of pain. They saw themselves on an expressway labeled "Terminal Fatigue" and wanted to know if there was an alternate route to the future.

I trace the roots of their weariness to a stereotype, which at first seems as ludicrous as if we were taking a paper tiger to task. But most who think through the progression agree that there is more reality in the pattern than they had previously acknowledged.

The story goes like this. In previous generations, the image of a church was one in which the elders (consistory, vestry, deacons, and so forth) gathered money in the treasury, went out, and hired a preacher. This employee of theirs delivered the sermon on Sunday and then, during the week, made hospital calls, was available for crises, showed up at the Lions Club to offer a prayer, or otherwise waited for the phone to ring. If there was need for a funeral or wedding, this pastor would be glad to attend to that as well.

The bottom line was that if anything needed to be done for God, the pastor was the hired hand who would do it. If a congregation did not guard itself it could become lazy, because its main activity was to give money and vote, while its pastor worked hard and was tired all the time.

Even in congregations that learned how to release lay leaders for ministry, the pastors were still expected to do much of the work of the church. Over time, as some churches grew very large, those patterns still remained, even though a lot more volunteers were helping out.

Now, enter the present. In my role as a consultant, I interviewed the staff of a church of 4,500. One of my assignments was to help the church think ahead to the future. So, based on the assumption that the church would continue to grow, I asked what I thought was a logical and predictable question: "What's this church going to look and feel like when it's nine thousand in size?"

The answer was almost a chorus: "Nine thousand!?" Everyone's voice carried a tone of disbelief. To underscore their response, one of them confirmed, "That's twice as big as we are now."

After an awkward silence, another staff member finally said, "If twice as big means twice as tired, Lord, let me out now." These people were stressed to the breaking point and could not imagine reaching a greater harvest in their city. They had not yet begun to operate on a level that allowed them breathing room for managerial and emotional refreshment.

Exceptional Talent and Extra-Mile Dedication

In my observations of large churches, a prime source of ministerial fatigue still traces back to a pastoral staff that operates under the model of pastors as primary caregivers. Whether unwittingly or not, ministers continue to train the parish to expect them to be available in ways that no human can consistently deliver.

As one example, an associate pastor in a church of some 6,000 people bumped into one of the church's long-term members in the hallway on Sunday morning. She confided that she was experiencing the messy breakup of a thirty-year marriage.

After responding with great empathy and concern, the pastor pulled out his appointment book and said, "I want you to know something. As a pastoral counselor on the staff of this church, I am behind you in this tragedy. I am putting your name right here at the very top of my list, and I want you to know that if you need us, we are here."

"Oh," she responded, "that is so comforting. Thank you very much." They prayed together, and she went home.

A few weeks later she had occasion to phone him, but he did not return her call. A couple of days later she left another message, but he still did not call back. After numerous unsuccessful attempts over a couple of weeks, she went to the church building and said to the receptionist, "Is Pastor Such and Such in?"

"Yes, but he can't receive any callers."

She nevertheless proceeded down the hall, found his office, walked in, and there was the dear man. On the credenza behind him were thirty-eight pink "While You Were Out" message slips laid in neat rows.

"Aren't you the same man," she began, "who said to me that because of the great trial I am undergoing and because of your availability to me I would not have to go through this alone? Didn't you put my name in your little black book, and didn't you tell me that you'd return my calls?"

He looked at her and said, "You don't seem to understand. I have thirty-eight calls here. Your call is fifth from the bottom of the pile. I have thirty-three other people I must call before I can get to you. I am working as hard as I know how. I'm putting in twelve- to fourteen-hour days. I'm covering the territory as quickly as possible, and I'm sorry to say that you'll just have to wait your turn!"

She walked out of his office, shattered and disillusioned. As it turned out, a laywoman in that church filled her need, from helping her deal with malpractice on the part of her attorney, to sitting with her in the courtroom during the long days of the trial, to taking her calls in the middle of the night as she wept her way, hour after hour, through all the adjustments.

Conventional wisdom says that this associate pastor ought to be taken out and flogged. But why? He loves people and genuinely wants to help them; that is why he entered the ministry. He voluntarily puts in overtime, which results in twelve- to fourteen-hour days, at no extra pay. He was taking very seriously the thirty-eight phone calls that had come his way.

How many victims are in this story? It's not just the woman going through a divorce. What about the wife and children of that staff member who, after fourteen hours, came home completely worn out? He was too beat to be a husband or a father. Was not the entire pastoral family a victim as well?

I submit that everyone was a victim and no one was the bad guy. I suggest that the villain was not a person but an insane idea that says it is possible for one person to be available to take care of 100, 200, 500, or 800 other people. The casualty was anybody living under that perfectly abominable notion.

What is the implication for a church trying to break the 800 barrier? Even extraordinary talent and extra-mile dedication cannot prevent eventual burnout. The pastor who sets up an "I am the caregiver" expectation by repeatedly saying, "Let me be your pastor," will sooner or later be pulled to the point of exhaustion.

> The first step toward a solution is to organize your time around delegating duties and training apprentices.

A necessary step to break the 800 barrier, the transition point most churches hit between 600 and 1,200, is to continually revise your estimate of what systems are required to see to it that your people receive the care they need. Remember, your faithfulness or unfaithfulness as a pastor is not measured in terms of fatigue.

The first step toward a solution is to organize your time around delegating duties and training apprentices. Until you become dispensable you cannot become promotable. God cannot hand you a new assignment if it would sink what He has already entrusted to you to oversee.

A second step is to rethink the organizational structure itself. Could improvements be made that would better ensure systemic spans of care? In the sections that follow, both of these steps will be fleshed out in greater detail.

Establish Reasonable Spans of Care

Properly managed spans of care are critical to a leader's effectiveness. The fundamental message that Jethro gave his son-in-law Moses was the wisdom in breaking an organization into smaller parts so that everyone could have an opportunity to be heard and have his or her questions addressed (see Exod. 18:13–23). A church, therefore, is most effective when it organizes itself around the spans of care that prove to be most manageable.

A lay pastor, under certain conditions, can typically run herd on about twenty names and can keep about ten people coming to a cell group. That assumes (1) the names are not a randomly selected, church-provided list but represent an affinity relationship among people already in the group; (2) this layperson has the help of both an apprentice leader and a host who takes care of the meeting location, refreshments, and the like; and (3) this layperson receives coaching, supervision, and encouragement on a regular basis. I explain very practically how to set up such a system in my book *Nine Keys to Effective Small Group Leadership*, which serves to focus attention on developing small group leaders and coaches and strengthening the caring connections among members.[1]

If lay ministers try to handle more people than that, they will, in most cases, run out of steam or they will neglect the needs of various members of their group. Once the group size exceeds about thirteen people, it will lose the qualities of intimacy, accountability, pastoral care, hands-on personal prayer, safety in self-disclosure, and surrogate extended-family support that the cell alone can deliver.

Instead, it becomes a class (15 to 25 people) or a congregation (25 to 150 people). General fellowship and a family-like feeling may be present, as well as acquaintance-making opportunities. The leadership will have opportunities to use their own spiritual gifts and train other leaders who are capable of leading additional groups.

But neither the class-sized group nor the congregation-sized group can hope to disciple most people with the quality of care they need.

If a church's goal is to make and multiply disciples of Jesus Christ, then it has two fundamental options: to use the effort and ministry of the professional clergy or to use the lay leadership. If the paid staff are the sole or primary agents for caring, they will always be weary and short. If an organization of lay volunteers is the agent, the care will be ever expanding and adequate—*if* the span of care for each can remain small enough to be effective.

Whom should the leaders in a beyond-800 church include in their personal spans of care? Other leaders, such as other staff members, the main church board, and those lay volunteers who have taken the responsibility to serve as coaches of lay pastors. By maintaining a leadership development focus within a reasonable span of care, a pastor can both avoid fatigue and continue leading the church to capture new growth opportunities.

Use Niche Marketing to Reach New People

In that regard, imagine that your church begins to experience and sustain a growth rate of ten new people a week. That translates into 400 a year. Five years from now, your cumulative influx will amount to 2,000 new people.

What, on the human level, would be necessary for that to happen? No matter what methodology you use, such as the list of sixteen methods in chapter 4, you will have to deal with certain stubborn realities to build a bridge between your church and your community.

Here are some general questions to ask as you seek how to unleash your church into your community or regional area:

1. Does your community perceive your church as a source of help? In other words, how does your church position itself in the eyes of the population segment you are targeting?

2. Does your community know who and what your church is? Do you have a clear strategy to interpret your church's program to your most susceptible population segments?

3. Can you scratch that itch? Do you know how to organize the resources of your church in such a way that you can fulfill the expectations of the market segment you are targeting?

4. Do you help people take part? As responding seekers come to church gatherings, what is your pathway for induction? Is there a clear route to membership and/or to greater levels of participation? Does it follow a progression that starts where they are now and gradually offers them higher challenges and more abundant opportunities for commitment?

5. Do your people experience vital Christianity? How does your church engender spiritual experience and formation? How does each meeting in your church, from the worship service to the senior adult travel club, contribute to this objective? In other words, how do faith, prayer, and other disciplines of the Christian life lead to transformed lives at each meeting these newcomers could be part of?

6. How does your church maintain a quality of community that provides care for all your people? All churches must deal with this issue, especially as they grow larger. How would your church complete the following sentence? "Everyone who wants to receive personal, pastoral-type care may do so through _____." Answers may range from "We offer one-on-one counseling" to "We're confident that, with all the programs we offer, you'll stumble upon something that gives you the care you need." I believe that the most workable, long-term solution is an intentional, carefully coached system of lay-led small groups. I introduced this idea in chapter 10 and will expand on it in chapter 13.

One of the privileges of a large church is that it has the talent and resources to market itself to very specific niches of a population. "Bridge events" can target special interests and offer additional entry points to the church. These might include, for example, a seminar offered by a Christian medical doctor on "Seven Keys for Coping with Stress," a workshop on how to teach English as a second language, a bunch of auto mechanics who bring their friends and get together at a local garage every Friday night to do car repairs for widows or single moms and others in need, and a youth group designed to appeal to the streetwise kids in the housing project down the street from the church building.

The most workable, long-term solution is an intentional, carefully coached system of lay-led small groups.

You can find several excellent resources that provide numerous insights and principles on marketing.[2] However, one of your goals should be not to advertise your merchandise but to merchandise your advertising. The Home Depot knows that come March, people will want to buy fertilizer for their gardens, and Target is aware that everyone is thinking about spring clothes for their children. So its stores already have the merchandise on display when the need arises. Likewise, a church needs to know its targeted population well enough to have anticipated its felt needs and be primed, prepared, and programmed to meet those needs in Jesus's name.

SELF-EVALUATION MOMENT

1. List twenty-five words or phrases that indicate why someone would want to attend a church.
2. Circle the words or phrases that indicate the felt needs *your* church is able to meet.
3. Put stars by the words or phrases that would particularly appeal to unchurched or unconverted people.

Divide by Age or Lifestyle

Recognizing the need for increased market targeting, most churches, by about 800, have already begun to reconfigure their staffs. In the previous chapter I described how a church of up to about 400 will develop a staff of specialists—a minister of music, Christian education, or outreach, for example. The larger church typically maintains the concepts of worship, fellowship, and education but also hires staff who will cover all three elements within one age group or life stage.

Each staff member, from youth minister to senior adults minister, receives the same assignment: "See to it that your age group comes to *worship* and has suitable program opportunities for *fellowship* and Christian *education*." These clergy, if given adequate resources and held accountable, can each carry 150 to 200 people. They typically sponsor large events, middle-sized gatherings, and small group meetings. The usual net effect is that each age group or life stage behaves like a little church; it accepts some people and excludes others; it takes good care of some and leaves others in the cold. Typically, more emphasis is placed on the teaching of intellectual concepts and on overall general fraternity than on the creation of intentional community.

A church such as this centers on the necessity of the congregation-sized structure and offers cells and classes as "nice to have" but not as necessities. Likewise, the celebration is a festival or convention of congregations, not a gathering of cells. The age- and life-stage targeting are healthy; the questionable notions are whether the congregation-sized group can be a primary-care structure or a significant entry port to the growth of the celebration.

The clergy of a congregation-centered church, though all quite busy, usually lack a purposeful plan for developing their lay leaders. The organizational chart for their church usually offers limited insight into who supervises whom, because it lists only the paid staff and identifies their relationship to the senior pastor or church board. As a result, a volunteer or part-time director of preschool ministry may oversee a staff that handles five hundred people, while the main responsibility of an ordained minister of singles may be one thirty-five-person class.

My point is not to demean someone whose ministry is smaller than another's (nor to be anticlerical). Rather I am highlighting the inefficiency that is frequently a part of this commonly accepted paradigm.

Another problem this type of church faces is that of structural fatigue. As a church continues to grow and begins to minister to thousands of people weekly, it will usually implement a matrix formula in which specialists support the generalists. For example, a minister of evangelism (specialist) will be brought on board and assigned to support all the ministers of age level (generalists) in developing outreach training and programming for their particular church-within-the-church.

In charting this progression (which I do in greater detail in my book *Prepare Your Church for the Future*[3]) and then researching it in hundreds of actual churches through my consulting work over the years, I have discovered that somewhere around 6,000 people, and perhaps as high as 12,000, the pastors fatigue and the church stops growing. In other words, the popularly used organizational formulas lead to most churches stalling somewhere between 6,000 and 12,000, as if they were a species of shrub that had reached its maximum height (see Figure 11).

Understand the Limits of Superchurches and Megachurches

As a result of faith, guts, and a feeder-receptor system (which will receive further comment in chapter 13), North American soil now boasts several thousand churches known as superchurches, with attendances between 1,000 and 2,000, and just over 1,500 even larger churches known as megachurches. Over fifty have consistently broken the 10,000 mark, and a handful have sustained growth beyond 20,000.[4]

Indeed, an increasing percentage of North American churches are becoming four- and five-digit entities. According to Lyle Schaller, between 1950 and 1990, the number of Protestant churches averaging

800 or more at worship tripled and perhaps quintupled.[5] Leadership Network's research confirms the continuing of this trend.[6] Such breakthroughs are reshaping the ecclesiastical landscape. Approximately one-fifth of churches on this continent account for one-half of all Protestant churchgoers.[7]

Figure 11

Organizational Choices
Determine Growth Ceilings

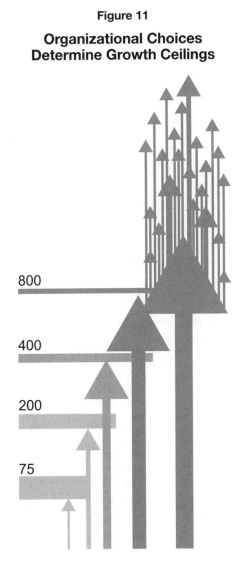

Enough knowledge of best practices is on hand to guide any church of 1,000 along this same path. How can you do it according to the currently used pattern highlighted in the previous chapter? (1) Rationalize your marketing by positioning your church as a source of help to a susceptible target population. (2) Manage your programming through giving age-group and life-stage assignments to your staff, and get the staff—rather than the board—to accept responsibility for planning and budgeting. (3) Shift your focus from that of a primary caregiver to that of a maker and coach of other caregivers. I have discussed this latter idea in virtually every chapter of the book, with this very specific recommendation: put the primary-care pastoral ministry of the church into the hands of lay shepherds who lead small groups.

These steps, prayerfully applied and directed by the Holy Spirit, can carry you beyond 1,000, but not without an eventual slowdown.

Could there be, however, an alternate path to the future that does not have the same theoretical size limits built in? What if, for example, each age-group or life-stage pastor were commissioned to focus his or her energies on developing a handful of lay leaders who would, in turn, coach a handful of lay leaders who would, in turn, care for the pastoral needs of that particular age group? Likewise, in the arena of corporate worship, what if a minister of celebrative arts were given the responsibility to produce lay ministry teams who would, in turn, lead the worship?

Put the primary-care pastoral ministry of the church into the hands of lay shepherds who lead small groups.

In other words, each of these pastors will be hired as a producer of other ministers rather than as a performer or primary caregiver (other than to a handful of lay leaders). For example, instead of having a minister of evangelism, now every staff member will be responsible for evangelism in every cell, because every cell is responsible for the evangelism of the people it assimilates.

The real church, then, is the cell-sized unit. Even the worship service is cell-driven in that it is a convention of cells. In this kind of church, a small group is not an add-on, like a new corner in a department store, to complement the youth department and the women's ministries department. Rather, the cell is the center of activity, and everything else is rationalized around it.

The cell is the center of activity, and everything else is rationalized around it.

This modification of structure, I believe, unlocks the terminal fatigue syndrome and uncaps the lid on maximum church size.

Offer Multiple Worship Services—and Multiple Sites

The simple questions, "Should we go to a second (or third, or fourth) worship service and/or should we become multisite (one church in two or more locations)?" frequently open the door to a host of related questions: What is the ideal size for our church? Do we want to expand our present ministries, extend ourselves through daughter churches, or both? Would our ministers and choir have the stamina for another service, or would other personnel be needed to fill the leadership spots? What long-cherished traditions and worship styles will be interfered with by an additional service?

Why go the multiple-worship-service route? Consider the following benefits:

1. You will allow the Holy Spirit, more than the city zoning board, to determine how great a harvest your church can reach. Not only will you overcome the vision limiter of "a full building means the harvest is complete for this year" (see chapter 2), but you will also circumvent the "no more growth" edicts of your zoning board when you try to enlarge your physical plant.

2. You will position yourself for growth, especially if the additional service "off-loads" the better attended 10:30 or 11:00

service. Lyle Schaller calls the multiple-service approach "the most effective means for increasing worship attendance."[8] John Vaughan says that 85 percent of growing churches are in what can be called a multiservice model.[9]

3. You will exercise optimal stewardship of the tens of thousands and even millions of dollars currently invested in your present facilities. Most church facilities are used, at best, at 20 percent of capacity. John Vaughan says, "My annual research of the 500 fastest-growing churches in the U.S. indicates that the wiser decision is to use the same space for a second, and then begin a third hour, if at all possible, before completing additional new buildings.[10] Those same ratios apply in any year going forward.

4. You will give additional laypeople a forum for ministry. Many times new talent cannot emerge because someone is already sitting in a given slot.

Instead of asking the same ushers to do double duty, why not discover how many new people would step forward to usher through a new team? Instead of recycling the band, choir, or regular instrumentalists, cultivate a handbell choir, a youth choir, a worship interpretative dance team, a single-adults a cappella group, or a children's glee club. Give them non-primetime exposure, and then when you feel both they and the congregation are ready, utilize them in your additional services. Lyle Schaller affirmed that for every 150 people in attendance, you have enough talent to develop an additional choir.[11]

Does the physical plant of your church stand idle on Monday night, Thursday night, Friday night, Saturday night, or Sunday afternoon? If a spiritual awakening came over all the unchurched people within a fifteen-minute drive of your church building, and they came to your church for help, you would need all kinds of alternate-hour services.

I propose that the missing ingredient in developing multiple worship services is not the lack of new people but the lack of compelling drive to reach an enlarged harvest, the lack of vision in how to raise enough lay talent to staff the additional services, and the lack of effective leadership that can do the political maneuvering necessary to rally the church in support of such new outreach.

Jack Hyles led First Baptist Church of Hammond, Indiana, to be the nation's largest church in the 1970s; during that decade, it held up to six rounds of Sunday school each Sunday. Willow Creek Community Church, in South Barrington, Illinois, which then became the nation's largest-attendance church for many years, offers weekend services designed for the seeker at the pace of two on Saturday night and two on Sunday morning, and then weeknight services designed for the believer on both Wednesday night and Thursday night.[12] Other churches hold several morning services in English and then host a Vietnamese, Korean, or Hispanic afternoon service.

The path to the future is already within your grasp, including your present financial resources. Who will step forward and take hold of these wonderful opportunities?

Are You Closer to the Future?

Leadership development is the core perspective for the ongoing health and growth of the larger church (see Figure 12). Disciples, not customers, are made a dozen or less at a time. Jesus's scenario was to pick twelve, fail one, and graduate eleven.

When you analyze the needs of your church or when you plan for the future, do you think primarily of individuals working alone or of an organizational grid that connects individuals through affinity-based groups? Do you see your church as a cluster of influence centers, each of whose particular ministry is shaped, guided, and directed by a specific leader?

The cell (or small group) system in most churches is like the fruit and vegetable bin in my refrigerator the week seedless grapes go on

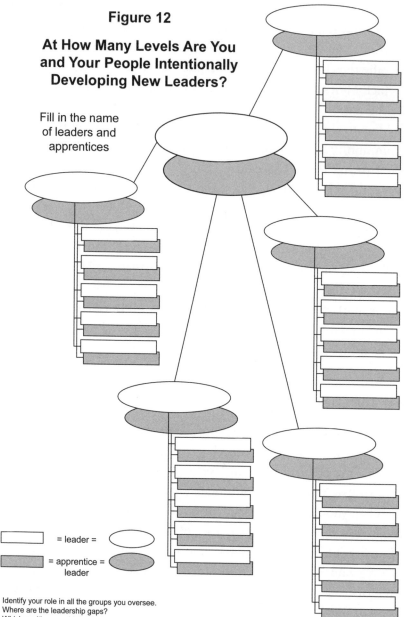

Figure 12

At How Many Levels Are You and Your People Intentionally Developing New Leaders?

Fill in the name of leaders and apprentices

☐ = leader = ◯
▓ = apprentice = ⬭
leader

Identify your role in all the groups you oversee.
Where are the leadership gaps?
Which positions are highest priority for apprenticeship training?

Leadership development is the core perspective for the ongoing health and growth of the larger church.

206

sale and my children have raided the kitchen ahead of me. All I can find are some loose grapes rolling around.

The cell system that takes a church beyond 800 is what the refrigerator bin looked like before my children arrived: overflowing with grapes and "structured" in such a way that when one of my kids grabbed an appropriate stem in the right place, virtually everything came with it.

Once you understand how all the "grapes" (representing affinity-based groups) plug in to one another at your church—how lay coaches hold each cluster together and how the staff are the stems that connect the clusters to one another—then you have a system to which you can provide effective guidance. Otherwise you are stuck dealing with loose grapes one at a time.

> *Leadership development is the core perspective for the ongoing health and growth of the larger church.*

If God is calling your church to be several times larger than you have previously imagined it could be, then you will plateau or stumble if you have to deal with one "grape" at a time. You need to find the stem on which a new social architecture can be constructed. You need a new set of tools to cope with the larger set of realities that you will soon experience.

The good news is that this toolset exists, it is as timeless as the principles of Scripture, and it is being modeled by a number of very exciting churches. The next chapter both describes and names that "new" paradigm.

FOR FURTHER THOUGHT

1. What are the evidences of ministry fatigue in your church? If God grants you an enlarged harvest, what needs to happen to prevent staff and key lay leaders from totally burning out?

2. How do you feel about the concept of "marketing" a church? In what ways could the publicity now generated by your church (brochures, radio broadcasts, Yellow Pages advertisements, street-side signs to promote vacation Bible school) be interpreted as marketing? What is the next step your church needs to take in its overall strategy to build bridges with the unchurched and unconverted?

3. Think of a beyond-800 church with which you are fairly well acquainted. Is it closer to being an undifferentiated mass unified around the charisma of the main pastor or an age-based or lifestyle-based set of churches within the big church? Why?

4. If your church has considered or implemented a multiple worship service format, what were the biggest snags in launching it? What is the greatest perceived benefit? What would need to happen for your church to launch and fill one more worship service than it is conducting now?

How to Break the Care Barrier

What is the next stage for the growing North American church? Some churches plant daughter churches, spin off satellite groups, or add multiple campuses and yet continue to maintain their numerical momentum. Some churches experience a change in pastors or other major transition and yet still keep increasing in scope and impact.

How do they do it? They grow bigger by becoming smaller. That's how they both reach and spiritually care for the abundant harvest that's around them—and likely around you as well.

More than one analyst has asked, "If the fields are so ripe, what's gone wrong with the harvest?" Why are 80 percent or more of United States and Canadian churches plateaued or declining?[1] Why does the average local church "face a tenuous future"[2] in an increasingly pluralistic and secular environment?

The Holy Spirit Is Being Underutilized

Our lack of greater impact stems, in part, from a widespread mistaken notion that I have tried to challenge in chapter after chapter of this book: that Western Christians, from long-term church members to lifetime denominational executives, assume that one person, because of an educational degree or an ordination certificate, is therefore rendered capable of meeting the spiritual and emotional needs of one hundred or more people. This solo caregiver professional pastor paradigm is a primary mechanism by which the Western church prevents itself from being a fully effective agent of God's redemption for our time.

Even Jesus acknowledged that a better system is needed. He told His disciples, "It is for your good that I am going away. Unless I go away, the Advocate will not come to you" (John 16:7). Jesus shifted His own ministry from that of person-to-person to a ministry of God-in-all through the Holy Spirit. On another occasion He promised, "Where two or three gather in my name, there am I with them" (Matt. 18:20).

This solo caregiver paradigm is a primary mechanism by which the Western church prevents itself from being a fully effective agent of God's redemption for our time.

The gift of the Holy Spirit makes it possible for a pastor to have confidence that the love, nurture, encouragement, and care God wishes for people to receive is available each time the Christian community comes together, whether that meeting is convened by ordained clergy or lay shepherds.

When you consider further the idea that each Christian is specially gifted by the Holy Spirit for the one-another ministry that builds up and matures the church (1 Cor. 12:1–12; 14:12, 26), then a new paradigm can be born. I propose that the church of the future—the church that wants to break the care barrier—will have this conviction at its heart: wherever Christians cluster together, the presence of Christ is there and adequate grace will be manifest to meet the needs of everyone present. In short, care for unlimited numbers of people is possible, because Jesus designed that idea as His better plan.

Many North American churches have acknowledged the importance of small groups where needs are met, accountability occurs, and more leaders are developed. Small, intimate settings were valued in eighteenth-century Britain in John Wesley's class meetings, in the nineteenth- and twentieth-century Sunday school movement, and the current cell church and small group groundswell evident everywhere.[3]

Care for unlimited numbers of people is possible, because Jesus designed that idea as His better plan.

Readers will understand that this book is primarily addressed to leaders of new or existing congregations who find themselves stuck at one point or another as they aspire to touch and incorporate those around them in an ever-expanding campaign for spiritual conversion and discipleship. Hundreds of thousands of congregations already exist, with pastors and facilities and histories of successful evangelization, who need the principles we are espousing here, even as new forms of congregation are being pioneered that do not utilize professional staff or facilities or programs.

Even as the number of very large churches and multisite mini-denominational churches are multiplying, in this millennium we are seeing another form of spiritual growth at the other end of the organizational size scale.[4] What is unprecedented since the early centuries of Christianity is the phenomena of networks of small groups that are being called "church planting movements." Globally, and recently in North America as well, networks of lay-led, Holy Spirit–dependent small groups are exploding in number. Hundreds and thousands of small group leaders, some newly converted, are accepting commissions to love God, love one another, and make disciples. Just as Asia was the inspiration for superchurches based on cells, Asia has also birthed the emerging model of networks of cells that exceed any recent imagination as to what is possible in terms of numerical growth. A new wave of understanding is promoted by David Garrison, author of *Church Planting Movements*; Steve Smith, whose book *T4T: A Discipleship Re-Revolution* describes the pioneering work of Ying Kai; and Curtis Sergeant, whose YouTube videos lay out the simplicity of a concept for networks of small and extremely simple churches.

Badge of Discipleship: One-Another Love

Whatever your church's size and current growth patterns, how do you prepare for an *expanded* availability of quality care? What structures best help a church flesh out Jesus's teaching that "by this everyone will know that you are my disciples, if you love one another" (John 13:35)?

One option is to hire more staff and clergy. Predictably, most churches run out of money long before they run out of needs. In fact, churches below one hundred in attendance are strongly moving in the direction of being led by self-supporting, bivocational clergy—or clergy who depend on income from a spouse or prior career. Economics are forcing it.

On top of that, the ratio of ministers to the total United States population is 1 to 714, hardly a feasible span of care, even if we could double or triple the current number of ordained ministers.[5]

How about training laypeople to serve as paraclergy on a volunteer basis, akin to the Stephen Series of one-to-one caregiving created by Kenneth Haugk?[6] This wonderful pastoral-care concept extends the caring capacity of professional ministry by preventing many care needs from going unmet, and sometimes serves more as a support system for overextended clergy than as a long-term answer to the needs of ever-growing congregations.

The solution advocated here, which enables the largest number of people to receive personal, quality attention, occurs when a church systematizes care by building it into the ongoing life of the entire fellowship. For this to happen, self-help caring must be developed as a mutual resource through a church-wide system of lay-led small groups. This idea echoes the solution to the "disaster area" analogy introduced at the beginning of chapter 1.

In short, the more caring cells your church has, the more people you can sustain and the more crises you can handle at a time without loss of quality. That means more people who will be able, in the name of Jesus Christ, to love a lost world and bring it to the Savior.

> *Adequate caring, fueled by Holy Spirit–given giftedness, lies at the foundation of all sustainable church growth.*

Adequate caring, fueled by Holy Spirit–given giftedness, lies at the foundation of all sustainable church growth.

Why Be Part of a Big Church?

We must come to realize that when a church grows to a four-, five-, or six-digit size it *could* mean that most of its people receive better care than they would in a smaller church. Its clergy leaders will have long ago abandoned the idea that they are the only, or even the best, primary caregivers. Such churches are, instead, organized around lay pastoral skills.

As a result, a second raison d'être is born: if someone has hopes of being a lay minister, this kind of church will not only *allow* such people to do so but will *encourage* and *empower* lay pastoring. The professional clergy will make it clear that the true heroes are laypeople, recruited and trained from within the church, who take responsibility for flocks of about ten. These lay pastors will ensure the spiritual nurture of the people in their cells in four ways: (1) they convene the group at least twice a month; (2) they set a tone in the group that conveys an openness to newcomers; (3) they, with the help from an apprentice leader, make sure their people receive care from one another outside the meetings; and (4) they meet regularly with someone designated to coach them on their various leadership questions or difficulties.

By contrast, the current North American phenomenon of the superchurch (1,000 to 1,999) and megachurch (2,000 and up) can be traced in too many cases to a feeder-receptor pattern of transfer growth from smaller churches.[7] An estimated 80 percent of all growth taking place in superchurches and megachurches comes through transfer, not conversion.[8]

People who desire anonymity find their way into smaller-sized churches that emphasize, instead of cells, one or more congregation-sized groups, such as a large adult Bible fellowship or a 150-person singles group.

As mentioned earlier, Dr. Yonggi Cho is founding pastor of the world's largest church, which reached and sustained an attendance of 625,000. The church traces its growth to the work of the Holy Spirit through some 35,000 trained lay pastors. As he explains:

> An estimated 80 percent of all growth taking place in superchurches and mega-churches comes through transfer, not conversion.

> The large church, through use of small groups, has proven to be uniquely able to be used by the Holy Spirit in our times. People in the small groups minister to each other in ways that they would ordinarily not. . . . And knowing they are all a part of the larger church gives each person a feeling of being a part of an ongoing work of God.[9]

I firmly believe that when any church adopts this system of home cell groups, it is going to grow.[10]

Prepare Your Church for the Future

Is there a name for a church organized around lay pastoral skills? This concept, when first announced, was reported by *Christianity*

Today in the pre-multisite era, to be "the most prominent on the contemporary church growth scene."[11] It gained widespread recognition under many names: church *of* small groups, cell-based church, cell-driven church, and leadership-development church, among others. My preference has been and is metachurch.

What does the term *metachurch* signify? One of the people who critiqued *Prepare Your Church for the Future*, the first book I wrote to explain the metachurch paradigm, said, "You're trying to describe what's coming next."

Exactly. Just as *meta*morphosis is the change of the caterpillar to butterfly, so *metachurch* emphasizes the changing character of the church and the new things God is bringing to pass.

The term alerts leaders to the radical differences in how ministry must be configured to deal with significant changes occurring in societies worldwide. The most fundamental of those alterations is the biological family that is not functioning well, where people are increasingly unable to find support, acceptance, belonging, positive role modeling, or a sense of normalcy.

The prefix *meta*, meaning "change," emphasizes a change in order or pattern in how the members of the family of God relate to one another. It also represents a significant shift in how ministry is perceived: that the clergy's critical task becomes leadership formation (developing more shepherds and coaches of these shepherds) rather than doing hands-on, primary-care ministry (being the church's only human shepherd). Finally, the term *metachurch* also represents an accompanying change in organizational priorities and structures.

What does a metachurch look like? It is a growing, usually multi-staff, local church committed to a joyous corporate worship of God (celebration), to formation of nurture groups and ministry teams led by lay pastors (cells), and to an organization of professionals and volunteers that focuses on development of leadership for ministry. It is also useful in the settings of the multisite churches that have begun multiplying in recent years.

As long as there is one person outside the fold, we cannot rest easy.

Is it any particular size? The metachurch concept represents a comprehensive approach to social architecture. It can begin at any attendance level.

How does it grow? In a metachurch, evangelism and discipleship become increasingly "cell driven" as believers use gifts of the Holy Spirit for one-another ministry through affinity-based, self-reproducing small groups. The metachurch paradigm allows unlimited numerical expansion without sacrificing quality; it is large enough to celebrate and small enough to care.

Why should a metachurch exist? Is the objective to break the 100,000 barrier or to conform to some new Asian or African definition of a successful church?

Metachurches are *not* motivated by size but to minister to hurting people (see Figure 13). Christians must not be satisfied as long as there is anybody who goes to bed at night crying himself or herself to sleep because of not knowing God's love. If we have to create larger churches, and even fill the landscape with 20,000-member churches for everyone to have an opportunity to be cared for, then that's one of the consequences of living as part of a world population of 7.3 billion people today, 8.5 billion by the year 2030, and 9.7 billion by the year 2050.[12]

As long as there is one person outside the fold, we cannot rest easy.

How Programmatic Thinking Skews Our Focus

Most people, including myself, would agree that the teaching in both mainline and evangelical churches in North America today is, taken as a whole, probably the finest quality of any time in history. We are blessed with more tools, skills, and resources, and a higher level in clergy education than in any previous era.

Rarely does a church exhibit a deficiency in teaching ability. Sometimes we find an inadequacy in teaching priority, but not in aptitude.

Figure 13

A "New" Approach
to Social Architecture

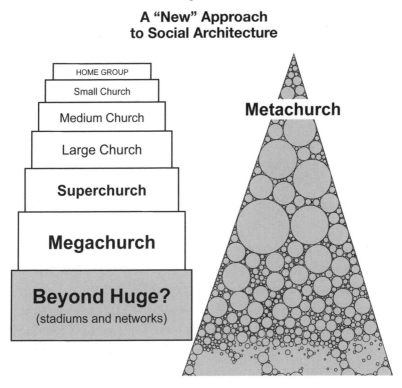

HOME GROUP

Small Church

Medium Church

Large Church

Superchurch

Megachurch

Beyond Huge?
(stadiums and networks)

Metachurch

Learning, however, is a different matter. North American pastors, lay leaders, and congregants believe many things to be true that, when examined closely, cannot be supported. This misinformation has little to do with the content of the Bible, the person of Jesus Christ, or other foundations to our grounding in God and in faith. Rather, our methodological truths sometimes undermine the passion and doctrine that motivate them.

In short, I believe that the educational process of today's church is far more shaped by American philosophies and methods of traditional public education than by the principles of Holy Writ. As such, a new paradigm, such as what metachurch thinking represents, cannot take root until people unlearn some of the programmed, curriculum-based assumptions at the core of North American ecclesiology.

217

I propose that the chief quality of an effective small group leader, and, in fact, the heartbeat of that cell ministry, is not the programmed organization or curriculum but a commitment to ministry where ministry settings are small enough that volunteer lay leaders can assure every participant will be cared for, listened to, and challenged in a warm and personal interaction among a group that is becoming friends and fellow travelers.

Why Not Merely "Append" Small Groups to the Present Structure?

The notion of lay-led cell groups is neither new nor unusual. However, groups are now seldom seen as an add-on program but are regarded as a seminal component of a church's vitality and health. The reorientation of a pastor's priorities to assure care through groups is not a mere cosmetic change in title.

The shift from programmatic, class-based instruction to relational, layperson-led cells begins in a pastor's mind. Learning to visualize how a church looks from the perspective of an ordinary participant requires a dramatic shift in thinking. But the more specific the mental picture, the more able the pastor will be to empower the system to empower the people to be tools in the hand of God (see Figure 14).

Whatever the pastor's vision is, people will catch it. A fuzzy concept translates into a foggy game plan. A clear, driving passion will be figured out by the key people of a church, even if the pastor does not articulate it.

The Critical Event at Your Church

What is the locus of ministry in your church? The Western church seems infatuated with the altar area, the pulpit, and the chairs surrounding the ordained minister as the epitome of "real" ministry.

Figure 14

Are You Waiting for Leaders to Arrive from Elsewhere, or Are You a Source of Leader Emergence?

	Transfer Approach	Metachurch Approach
Where do most new leaders come from?	Developed elsewhere.	Developed locally.
Who initiates their development?	1. Already-developed leaders who are persuaded to wear an additional "hat" (unless they're already burned out). 2. Already-developed leaders who are willing to trade "hats." 3. Newly transferred Christians from other churches.	1. New believers. 2. Inactive or "warehoused" Christians.
How big is the volunteer pool you can draw from?	Fixed. (It's limited to the number of already-trained Christians in your church plus other area churches.)	Ever expanding. (It's limited only by the size of your church's "harvest" vision.)
What's the best age-profile of a volunteer leader?	All ages, both single and married, though the most strategic are nesting-stage parents, especially those with children ages 3–15.	Same.
How does a church typically build staff to support its volunteer leaders?	Departmentalizing pattern. (The church typically brings on staff for youth, then children, then senior adults [if an older church], then single adults, then various parenting stages such as single parents, young parents, nesting-stage parents, and empty-nest parents.)	Districting pattern. (The church typically identifies whatever age groups have the most cell-group participants—often nesting-stage parents—and then hires or develops staff to support them.)
What's the long-term impact?	1. The primary volunteer pool gets overlooked. 2. There is only a small "zero-sum" pool of volunteer candidates. You are limited to the "cream of the crop" of your already-developed leaders.	1. The primary volunteer pool gets the most attention. 2. The pool of potential leaders is virtually unlimited, i.e., it's the population of the service area compared to the number of group leaders your church has developed.

The metachurch suggests that the great harvest to which Christians are called requires a new location for the "critical event" in the life of a church.

Take the McDonald's hamburger chain as an illustration. To organize a successful McDonald's restaurant, two important steps must take place. First, a would-be franchiser has to be shown that it makes sense to invest in McDonald's. Otherwise this financier will not put up the capital necessary to erect the building. Second, the franchiser must be trained to make the counter person a hero in the system.

> Whatever the pastor's vision is, people will catch it. A fuzzy concept translates into a foggy game plan.

The general public has no contact with the franchiser. In fact, they have no interest in the name or personality of anyone in management. The person who makes a difference to their world is the one who stands behind the counter and says, "How may I help you?" Thus the one role in the whole McDonald's system that most determines whether or not you will return is that of the counter person.

The critical social event in the entire McDonald's chain, as far as the customers are concerned, is the five-minute wait from the time they hit the door until they walk away with their steaming hot cheeseburgers and fries. (I assume a constant in the cleanliness of the site and quality of the food.)

In other words, if you stand at that stainless steel counter, receive what you asked for, and then leave with your need met within your monetary budget and time limit, you are likely to come back again and again. Likewise will millions of other people who experience the same favorable results. As far as you are concerned, you do not care what happens in the boardroom or at the franchiser fair. The entire McDonald's system is engineered to see to it that a smiling counter person can deliver what you expect.

It is now very apparent that churches can create a similar locus of ministry, which could impact the North American spiritual seeker in a similarly positive and appealing manner. What if your church's goal were that every person within the influence of your community had the opportunity to be in touch with about ten other people, both in one-on-one experiences and in the context of a small, loving, caring small group? That encounter would open the door to a natural progression. When people are able to develop trust and feel well treated, they conclude, *If this group of people is able to love me, as unloving as I am, then the God who sent them must be a loving, personal God too.*

> What if your church's goal were that every person within the influence of your community had the opportunity to be in touch with a small, loving, caring small group?

The metachurch takes the most plentiful talent we have—one person in ten—and asks that individual, by the aid of the Holy Spirit in mutual ministry of the saints, to provide a safe place for people to come to Christ, to ask their questions, to grow, to confess their sins, to find absolution, and to find encouragement. That is the critical event. Everything else in the system had better contribute to it.

The critical event in a metachurch, then, revolves around the intimacy of the family unit or spiritual-kinship unit facilitated by a lay minister who has a limited span of care (about ten people) and who has access to training in the social and leadership skills necessary to pull this off and to replicate himself or herself through an apprentice.

That means the baker, the truck driver, the salad maker, the franchiser, the shift leader, and the personnel at McDonald's corporate headquarters must not lose sight of the fact that the critical event must be supported.

Am I suggesting that the pulpit event is no longer necessary? No. A message, even a scholarly one, can be very helpful in identifying and understanding the truths of Scripture.

While the role of the sermon is significant, it stands in the same relationship to the critical task of caring as a franchiser stands in relation to the McDonald's counter person. It is a necessary step but not the only one. Preaching, therefore, is not the end of your responsibility and thus cannot be considered the only critical event in the life of a church.

The fruit of a metachurch pastor is not the shepherd's role of helping another Christian but rather the minister-maker's role of forming another Christian into a leader who, in turn, is capable of training another leader. This is precisely the concept that Paul teaches his apprentice in 2 Timothy 2:2.

In other words, a metachurch pastor will shepherd other shepherds: the staff and volunteer leaders who can, in reciprocal fashion, reproduce themselves in others. Through the process dozens, hundreds, and even thousands of others receive pastoral care. That is what ranching is all about.

Three Paths into an Assured Care Infrastructure

When initially proposing how to multiply lay leaders and encourage them to become caregivers, I advocated launching groups with willing volunteers who were instructed and coached in duplicating themselves by recruiting apprentices. That is a steady and sure approach that can work in any congregation. It was followed when Willow Creek Community Church began its implementation of small groups as Bill Hybels directed his staff to focus on assuring care to that legendary congregation. You'll find their principles of small-group adaptation in *Building a Church of Small Groups: A Place Where Nobody Stands Alone* and also *Leading Life-Changing Small Groups*, both by Bill Donahue, their director of small groups at the time. He also created several training manuals. About that time I developed the book *Nine Keys to Effective Small Group Leadership*, designed to focus attention on developing small group leaders and coaches and strengthening the caring connections among members.

In Southern Baptist circles, with the encouragement of Lifeway Resources, churches have renamed many of their Sunday school classes as on-campus Sunday morning small groups, and with weekly circles and "cottage" prayer meetings renamed as home-based small groups. The shift from instructional formatted meetings toward more relational settings quieted the contention between Sunday school and small group advocates with widespread benefits. In such settings, believers are directed to participate in weekly "big church" worship, intimate small-groups, and a third point of participation in some serving role. A popular book that encourages this focus is Thom Rainer and Eric Geiger's *Simple Church: Returning to God's Process for Making Disciples.*

In Southern California, at Saddleback Church, Rick Warren invited Brett Eastman from Willow Creek to foster a small group care system that could cover the entirety of Saddleback's 30,000 adherents. Brett worked with Rick to create a short DVD series suitable for playback in a living room and offered the videos to anyone willing to host a small gathering in their home, insert the disc, push the *play* button, and watch together. Year after year, campaigns that promote hosting for six weekly home-based meetings have grown, until the number of people attending a small group during a campaign has surpassed the typical weekly worship attendance at Saddleback. Leaders and members who are exposed to these hosted small groups often become continuing group leaders and care for their people throughout the year. Saddleback's pastor of small groups, Steve Gladen, describes the entire journey toward small groups in his book *Small Groups with Purpose: How to Create Healthy Communities.*

Enter the Future Now

The number of people who do *not* claim to be Christians is numerically greater today than ever.[13] Translation? The harvest fields are just outside our door as never before.

The next person, or ten, or one hundred, or one thousand who come to Christ in the context of your church could be the finest and most leadership-skilled saints you will ever have the privilege of training. Much will depend on whether you decide to empower them through enrollment as leaders or disempower them by affirming their role as your adoring fans.

Consider this as your prayer and resolution: "Dear God, which people in my community would You be pleased to draw to Yourself through the enfolding arms of our church? I will, by Your grace, see to it that every person who comes our way has the opportunity to be well cared for in a group of no larger than ten. I will pay the price to train and multiply the number of cell-group leaders necessary so that these newcomers can be personally encouraged and matured in their walk with You."

If that prayer reflects the intention of your heart, I predict you will see a transformation in your ministry and in the lives of your people that exceeds any dream you have been able to put together to this point.

The reason? You no longer attempt, on the basis of your availability, to be a super pastor, super staff member, or super lay leader. Instead, your vision is that of tapping into the gift of the Holy Spirit, who indwells every believer in your church. You will confidently seek out and train those people who have a God-given leadership ability to nurture the spiritual lives of newcomers. And you will work with them to develop the apprentices necessary for the next generation of leadership.

If church leaders can firmly grasp this idea, they can evangelize our cities to the very margins. The follow-up gaps will disappear. The alienation and despair that people now feel will be transformed into hope and confident lives of faith. And broken and wounded families will be rebuilt as people are reparented in the context of spiritual kinship groups.

The net result is that you will experience a blessing from God that exceeds anything you have ever hoped for, imagined, or dared to pray for.

When the pastors I coached asked for my help in training their lay leaders, I wrote a book that specifically focuses on what lay leaders need to know and do to be effective small group leaders: *Nine Keys to Effective Small Group Leadership*. It is available in paperback and ebook at Amazon.com.

Are you asking God to break the growth barriers in your church? Do you have the capacity to believe that you are capable of leading growth in your church? As soon as you get the answers to those questions straight, your church will grow.

It is as simple—and as hard—as that.

FOR FURTHER THOUGHT

1. What concept in this chapter registers most deeply with your spirit? Which do you find to be most troublesome?

2. Is the Holy Spirit being underutilized in your church? Why or why not?

3. Have you read about, visited, or known of a metachurch? What ministries are you aware of in your community that are in the early stages of changing over to this paradigm?

4. What is the situation in your church at present as to whether preaching is the critical event or lay pastoring is the critical event? How would the McDonald's illustration apply to the structures of your church?

5. As a result of reading and praying through this book, what is God calling you to do and to be? Why? What is the next step for you to take?

Acknowledgments

This book is dedicated to those pastors, lay leaders, and church and mission executives with whom we have had the privilege of working over the years through various consultations, seminars, phone conversations, and emails. You have influenced, impressed, and taught us in more ways than this page could possibly express.

It takes a great deal of courage to face the pain that accompanies change, for in the breaking of every barrier there must be the willingness, akin to that of an Olympic athlete, to press the limits of personal endurance. Without such risk, a person remains within borders that are too calm to be challenging.

None of us has approached the issue of church growth without an armful of experiences, biases, and dreams. Our questions are not merely "What would be ideal?" but "What is the next perspective or specific step that would make the greatest difference in our moving toward that ideal?"

In that quest for hardiness, for the will to implement what we know as wisdom, we could not have written this book without the example of the many "championship players" who are making a significant contribution to the well-being of others, including ourselves.

Many thanks also to all who read this revised and updated manuscript at various stages and offered both encouragement and valuable critique: Jon Benzinger, Robert D. Black Jr., Matthew Hooper, Brad Leach, Geoffrey Mitchell, Scott Nichols, Sunday Ogidigbo, and Jeremy Roberts.

Our thanks as well to the talented artist David Rodriguez of www .drgorilla.com, who took our original graphics to a whole new level.

Questions about Reprints

Whenever charts or other visuals are used in a book, questions inevitably arise from readers who want to understand more about how copyright law applies to their particular situation. Here is how the permission issue works for *How to Break Growth Barriers*. Individuals purchasing this book are allowed to reproduce the graphics for not-for-profit uses in a local church. Quotations from the text, of up to 150 words, may also be used without special authorization in reviews, bulletin inserts, seminar notebooks, overhead transparencies, and other printed media.

Otherwise, written permission from the copyright holder (the author) *is necessary* to reproduce the illustrations or any other parts of this book in films, videotapes, books, magazines, denominational publications, or any other form. For further information, please contact the author via the publisher as follows.

Foreign-language translations are likewise prohibited under international copyright law to protect the integrity of the book's content. To obtain written permission for translation and assistance in contextualizing the content, contact:

Baker Publishing Group
P.O. Box 6287
Grand Rapids, MI 49516-6287
Phone: (616) 676-9185
www.bakerbooks.com

Notes

Chapter 1 What Can This Book Do for You?

1. The word *systemic*, used here, accentuates interrelationships and the fact that one part of a system affects the whole. This idea is slightly different from the word *systematic*, which refers to how the system is ordered and organized. I develop this comparison further in the opening paragraphs of chapter 4.

2. Throughout this book, I use the word *church* to indicate a local body of believers (Bronx Christian Alliance Church) or the sum of all churches (the church as the body of Christ). The word *church* always refers to people, not their place of worship—which I term *church building* or *church facility*.

The word *congregation* in this book is not synonymous with the word *church*. *Congregation*, rather, will signify a certain middle-sized group, which is bigger than a home-based cell group and smaller than a church-wide worship celebration.

Peter Wagner, in *Your Church Can Grow* (rev. ed. Ventura, CA: Regal, 1984), first popularized the nomenclature of *cell*, *congregation*, and *celebration* (see especially pp. 111–26). My book *Prepare Your Church for the Future* (Revell: 1991) develops the implications of each particular size gathering.

3. Lyle E. Schaller first popularized the concept of "ranching" that this book addresses, which we often voice as "coaching." Writing on the issue of a minister's leadership style, Schaller compares two images of the role of the pastor. "The more common image is of the shepherd who is directly concerned about and personally involved with each member of the flock. A radically different image is reflected by the comment of the senior minister of a large Presbyterian congregation in Texas: 'When you're the pastor of a congregation as large as this one,' he explained, 'you can't be a shepherd; you have to be a rancher!'" (Lyle E. Schaller, *Survival Tactics in the Parish* [Nashville: Abingdon, 1977], 51.)

In a later book that addresses the church of 450 to 700 in worship attendance, which he calls a ranch, Schaller says: "One of the most important responsibilities of the senior minister is to help the members, and especially the lay leadership, realize this is a ranch and must be operated like a ranch. . . . The primary responsibility of the rancher is to see that larger picture, to operate within a long time frame that is appropriate for a ranch and to resist the pressures (and often the temptation) to plunge in and 'do it myself.' The rancher spends less time 'doing' and more time making sure the job gets done (by someone else) than does the gardener or housekeeper." (Lyle E. Schaller, *Looking in the Mirror: Self-Appraisal in the Local Church* [Nashville: Abingdon, 1984], 31.) See also Lyle E. Schaller, *Growing Plans: Strategies to Increase Your Church's Membership* (Nashville: Abingdon, 1983), 93–94.

4. Bill Easum and Bill Cornelius, *Go Big: Lead Your Church to Explosive Growth* (Nashville: Abingdon, 2006), 62, 10, 1, 5.

5. Bill M. Sullivan, *Ten Steps to Breaking the 200 Barrier* (Kansas City, MO: Beacon Hill Press, 1988), 14.

6. Eddie Gibbs, *I Believe in Church Growth* (Grand Rapids: Eerdmans, 1982), 313, 380–84.

7. Schaller, *Survival Tactics*, 52–53.

8. Harry H. Fowler, *Breaking Barriers of New Church Growth* (Rocky Mount, NC: Creative Growth Dynamics, 1988), 55–56.

9. Wagner, *Your Church Can Grow*, 52, 77. See also C. Peter Wagner, writing in the foreword to *A Caring Church*, by Charles A. Ver Straten (Grand Rapids: Baker, 1988):

> Too many churches today expect the ministry of the church to be done by the pastor, not by the people of God. . . . The bulk of the pastoral work of the church can and should be done by laypeople. . . .
>
> On the sheep ranch it is obvious that the only way large numbers of sheep can be adequately cared for is to break them down into smaller bands of sheep assigned to one shepherd. It does not require a degree in organizational management to recognize the wisdom of such structuring. Jethro advised Moses to do it back in the days of the Exodus. . . .
>
> Research has shown that a chief cause of burnout has been the tendency of pastors falling into the trap of not being able to say *no* to demands on their time. No pastor wants to say no to a church member who is hurting and who needs pastoral care. How . . . can a pastor say *yes* to any and all who need help without entering the burnout syndrome? By delegating the ministry of pastoral care to gifted and trained church members who—believe it or not—can often do a better job at it than the senior pastor could!
>
> True evangelism brings people to Christ and also into the body of Christ. . . . Unless the members of the body are mobilized to do the ministry of the church, the growth of the church will be limited. At least 80 percent of USA churches are under 200 in attendance. One of the major reasons for this is that the members of those churches unwisely demand that their pastor do all the ministry of the church. A pastor can do all the ministry, but only up to the 200 barrier. If new members are going to be brought into the church and if it is to cross the 200 barrier, it is essential to develop lay shepherding ministries.

Finally, see C. Peter Wagner, *Church Planting for a Greater Harvest* (Ventura, CA: Regal, 1990), 113–14:

> The shepherd mode . . . can function well up to the 200 barrier, but not above it. Pastors whose job satisfaction depends heavily on a shepherding ministry are typically small church pastors.
>
> A rancher mode can take the church through the 200 barrier. The essential difference between the shepherd and the rancher is not whether the sheep are cared for—they are in both cases if things are going as they should. The difference is who takes care of the sheep. The shepherd must do it personally; the rancher delegates the pastoral care to others.

10. Charles Chaney and Ron Lewis, *Design for Church Growth* (Nashville: Broadman, 1977), 53, 55.

11. Gary L. McIntosh, *Taking Your Church to the Next Level: What Got You Here Won't Get You There* (Grand Rapids: Baker, 2009), 15, 116.

12. Elmer L. Towns, John N. Vaughan, and David J. Seifert, *The Complete Book of Church Growth* (Wheaton: Tyndale, 1981), 234–37.

Chapter 2 How Can You Enlarge Your Vision?

1. Peter F. Drucker, *The Effective Executive* (New York: Harper & Row, 1985), 113. See also Peter F. Drucker, *Managing the Non-Profit Organization* (New York: HarperCollins, 1990).

2. For further information on clergy salaries, see chapter 11, note 4.

3. Lyle E. Schaller, *Hey, That's Our Church!* (Nashville: Abingdon, 1975). See also Schaller, *Growing Plans*, 169; Lyle E. Schaller, *The Small Church Is Different!* (Nashville: Abingdon, 1982), 81; and Dallas Willard, *The Spirit of the Disciplines: Understanding How God Changes Lives* (San Francisco: Harper & Row, 1988).

4. Bill Hybels, *Too Busy Not to Pray: Slowing Down to Be with God* (Downers Grove, IL: InterVarsity Press, 1988), 101–6.

Chapter 3 How Does Vision Motivate?

1. Warren Bennis and Burt Nanus, *Leaders: Strategies for Taking Charge* (New York: Harper & Row, 1985).

Also, for an integrated Christian perspective, see Merrill J. Oster, *Vision-Driven Leadership* (San Bernardino, CA: Here's Life Publishers, 1991).

2. David Yonggi Cho with Harold Hostetler, *Successful Home Cell Groups* (Plainfield, NJ: Logos International, 1981). See also my analysis of Dr. Cho's ministry in *Prepare Your Church for the Future,* 52–53, 134, 213–18.

3. For help in identifying your church's vision, framing it in a compelling way, and setting achievable short-term and long-term goals to implement it, see Will Mancini and Warren Bird, *God Dreams: 12 Vision Templates for Finding and Focusing Your Church's Future* (Nashville: LifeWay, 2016).

4. Michael LeBoeuf, *The Greatest Management Principle in the World* (New York: Putnam, 1985), 23, 136–37.

5. Loren Cunningham with Janice Rogers, *Is That Really You, God?* (Seattle: YWAM Publishing, 1984), 55.

6. This section, including the terms *outcome*, *blockage*, and *action*, draws its insight from an unpublished manuscript by David Lueke, a Lutheran pastor, seminary leader, author, and friend from whom I have learned much.

7. Joel Arthur Barker, *Future Edge: Discovering the New Paradigms of Success* (New York: William Morrow, 1992), 163.

8. Max DePree, *Leadership Is an Art* (New York: Doubleday, 1989), 9. See also George Barna, *The Power of Vision* (Ventura, CA: Regal, 1992).

9. See the last section of chapter 10 for an extended explanation of church facilities issues.

10. A number of diagnostic tools are available. For the Myers-Briggs approach see Isabel Briggs Myers and Mary H. McCaulley, *Manual: A Guide to the Development and Use of the Myers-Briggs Type Indicator* (Palo Alto, CA: Consulting Psychologists Press, 1985) and David Kiersey and Marilyn Bates, *Please Understand Me: Character and Temperament Types* (Del Mar, CA: Prometheus, 1984).

Chapter 4 How Would an Outsider Describe Your Church?

1. Cited in Wagner, *Your Church Can Grow,* 47. See McGavran's related discussion in chapter entitled "Methods Which Multiply Churches" in Donald A. McGavran, *How Churches Grow: New Frontiers of Mission* (New York: Friendship Press, 1959), 122–31.

2. Wagner, *Your Church Can Grow*, 46.

3. Carl George with Warren Bird, *Prepare Your Church for the Future* (Grand Rapids: Revell, 1991), 26–41.

Chapter 5 How Strong Is Your Growth Bias?

1. See the opening pages of chapter 10 for a more detailed breakdown of typical church sizes.

Chapter 6 Why Develop the Skills of a Caregiving Coach?

1. Derek J. Tidball, *Skillful Shepherds: An Introduction to Pastoral Theology* (Grand Rapids: Zondervan, 1986), 104–14.

2. Bill Hull, *The Disciple Making Pastor* (Grand Rapids: Revell, 1988), 190–202; cf. 74–103, 174–89. See also A. B. Bruce, *The Training of the Twelve* (repr. Grand Rapids: Kregel, 1971). For a biblical theology of equipping, based on a paradigm supportive of a ranching perspective, see Greg Ogden, *The New Reformation: Returning the Ministry to the People of God* (Grand Rapids: Zondervan, 1990), 96–116.

3. For theological analysis of a dependency model, see Ogden, *The New Reformation,* 86–137. For iconoclastic, even sassy, theological analysis, see chapter 7, "Luther Went Too Soon" by Gene Edwards and Jim Rutz in *The Open Church*, ed. Jim Rutz (Augusta, ME: 1992).

4. In my book *Prepare Your Church for the Future,* 42–54, I describe a "zoo" of church sizes from mouse to dinosaur. Each level has special characteristics and requires a different style of leadership.

5. See Elton Trueblood, *The Incendiary Fellowship* (New York: Harper & Row, 1967), 34–54.

Chapter 8 Should You Use More Than One Leadership Style?

1. For a different version of the berry bucket theory, which emphasizes how to work with senior formerberries, see chapter 10 of Carl F. George and Robert E. Logan, *Leading and Managing Your Church: Effective Management for the Christian Professional* (Tarrytown, NY: Revell, 1987).

2. Lyle E. Schaller, *Activating the Passive Church: Diagnosis and Treatment* (Nashville: Abingdon, 1961), 137–41.

Chapter 9 Multiply by Releasing

1. Melody Beattie, author of the *New York Times* bestseller *Codependent No More* (San Francisco: Harper/Hazelden, 1987), defines a codependent by quoting recovery pioneer Earnie Larsen: "Those self-defeating learned behaviors or character defects that result in diminished capacity to initiate, or participate in, loving relationships." These and other definitions come from Melody Beattie, *Beyond Codependency: And Getting Better All the Time* (San Francisco: Harper/Hazelden, 1989), 12.

2. David Johnson and Jeff VanVonderen, *The Subtle Power of Spiritual Abuse* (Minneapolis: Bethany, 1991), 68.

3. The Roman Missal, Eucharistic Prayer IV, verses 25–30. For background and commentary see Raymond Maloney, *Our Eucharistic Prayers in Worship, Preaching and Study* (Wilmington, DE: Michael Glazier, 1985), 66.

4. See Tim Stafford, "The Hidden Gospel of the 12 Steps," *Christianity Today* vol. 35 no. 8 (July 22, 1991): 14–19; See also Michael G. Maudlin, "Addicts in the Pew: Interview

with Dale Ryan," *Christianity Today* vol. 35 no. 8 (July 22, 1991): 12–21; and *Twelve Steps for Christians* (San Diego: Recovery Publishing, 1988).

Chapter 10 How to Break the 200 Barrier

1. The theological foundation for church growth is summarized in C. Peter Wagner, *Strategies for Church Growth: Tools for Effective Mission and Evangelism* (Ventura, CA: Regal, 1987), 17–131. More detailed systematic justifications of the church growth movement are in Gibbs, *I Believe in Church Growth*; C. Peter Wagner's *Church Growth and the Whole Gospel: A Biblical Mandate* (New York: Harper & Row, 1981); and Ebbie Smith, *Balanced Church Growth* (Nashville: Broadman, 1984).

2. Some excellent resources that can help the smaller church begin to experience a growth momentum are C. Wayne Zunkel, *Growing the Small Church: A Guide for Church Members* (Elgin, IL: David C. Cook, 1983); C. Wayne Zunkel, *Growing the Small Church: A Guide for Church Leaders* (Elgin, IL: David C. Cook, 1982); Carl S. Dudley, *Making the Small Church Effective* (Nashville: Abingdon, 1978); Carl S. Dudley and Douglas Alan Walrath, *Developing Your Small Church's Potential* (Valley Forge, PA: Judson Press, 1988); Harry H. Fowler, *Breaking Barriers on New Church Growth* (Rocky Mount, NC: Creative Growth Dynamics, 1988); Sullivan, *Ten Steps to Breaking the 200 Barrier*; and Lyle E. Schaller, *Forty-Four Ways to Increase Church Attendance* (Nashville: Abingdon, 1988).

3. This is Lyle E. Schaller's observation as well in *Activating the Passive Church: Diagnosis and Treatment* (Nashville: Abingdon, 1981), 25–26, and *Growing Plans*, 11.

4. Church consultants use a number of tools for keeping score: average worship attendance of adults only, average worship attendance of adults and children, peak worship attendance (such as Easter or Christmas Eve), Sunday school average attendance, Sunday school membership, baptized membership, confirmed membership, total membership, and resident membership, just to name a few.

This book focuses on average worship attendance of adults and children (total nose count) because this particular tally offers one of the most accurate barometers, both predictive and descriptive, of church personality, style, and sociological characteristics. See also the comment on comparing membership to attendance in note 7 of this chapter.

5. This number comes from academic groups that have studied various ways of calculating the total number of Protestant churches, such as the Hartford Institute for Religion Research, www.hartfordinstitute.org.

6. Several national studies have each found a number about this size. This calculation comes from the Faith Communities Today project, in their "American Congregations 2015" report, http://www.faithcommunitiestoday.org/sites/default/files/American-Congregations -2015.pdf. The specific examples in this chapter's charts update and confirm the accuracy of the data but also illustrate the wide variance between denominations.

7. Size statistics are based on 2014 data from a cross section of denominations (large, small, mainline, evangelical, charismatic, and so forth), all based on weekend worship attendance. It is extremely difficult, however, to correlate membership with attendance. In some churches, particularly those in the holiness traditions, attendance may be higher than membership. In others, particularly long-established mainline churches, membership may be two to five times higher than attendance.

8. See chapter 3, note 6 on annual 100 largest churches statistics.

9. Wagner, *Church Planting for a Greater Harvest*, 130.

10. Ibid., 131. One of the first writers to develop this concept was Carl Dudley, *Making the Small Church Effective*, 32–35.

11. Quoted by Russell Chandler in *Racing Toward 2001: The Forces Shaping America's Religious Future* (Grand Rapids: Zondervan, 1992), 292. Emphasis is Mr. Chandler's.

12. Elmer Towns, *Ten of Today's Most Innovative Churches: What They're Doing, How They're Doing It, and How You Can Apply Their Ideas in Your Church* (Ventura, CA: Regal, 1990), 243.

13. For details and examples see my book *Prepare Your Church for the Future*, especially pages 122–29.

Chapter 11 How to Break the 400 Barrier

1. See chapter 9 for a discussion of ministers' dysfunctional households. For an application of family-systems insights to church staff relationships, see Anne Marie Nuechterlein, *Improving Your Multiple Staff Ministry: How to Work Together More Effectively* (Minneapolis: Augsburg, 1989).

2. See chapter 9, note 1, for a definition of codependency.

3. Lyle E. Schaller, *Parish Planning* (Nashville: Abingdon, 1971), 38–46, 63. See also Lyle E. Schaller and Charles A. Tidwell, *Creative Church Administration* (Nashville: Abingdon, 1975), 45–54, 62–65; Lyle E. Schaller, *Forty-Four Ways to Revitalize the Women's Organization* (Nashville: Abingdon, 1990), 76–77; and Lyle E. Schaller, *Create Your Own Future: Alternatives for the Long-Range Planning Committee* (Nashville, Abingdon, 1991), 26, 59.

4. For church-related salary and compensation planning, many denominations publish "how to determine compensation" type books. See also Richard R. Hammar, *2016–2017 Compensation Handbook for Church Staff* (Church & Clergy Tax, 2015). For larger churches (attendance of 500 to 50,000) see Leadership Network's extensive library of free downloads at www.Leadnet.org/salary.

5. See Kenneth K. Kilinhski and Jerry C. Wofford, *Organization and Leadership in the Local Church* (Grand Rapids: Zondervan, 1973), 174. See also Charles E. Tidwell, *Church Administration—Effective Leadership for Ministry*, rev. ed. (Nashville: Broadman, 1991), 114–15.

6. See Warren Bird, "12 Salary Trends Every Church Leader Should Know: 2016 Large Church Salary Study—Executive Summary," *Leadership Network*, September 26, 2016, available for free download at leadnet.org/salary.

7. I discuss the development of contemporary staffing patterns according to church size in my book *Prepare Your Church for the Future*, 42–54.

8. Drucker's emphasis on working from strength is highlighted in "Managing to Minister: An Interview with Peter Drucker," *Leadership* vol. 10 no. 2 (Spring 1989): 18. His definition of good management comes from *The Effective Executive* (New York: Harper & Row, 1985), 71, where he says: "To make strength productive is the unique purpose of organization. It cannot, of course, overcome the weaknesses with which each of us is abundantly endowed. But it can make them irrelevant."

9. For a biblical and church-oriented perspective on delegation, see Carl F. George and Robert E. Logan, *Leading and Managing Your Church* (Tarrytown, NY: Revell, 1987), especially chapter 7, "Developing People through Delegation." Also Myron Rush, *Management: A Biblical Approach* (Wheaton: Victor, 1983); Stephen Douglas et al., *The Ministry of Management* (San Bernardino, CA: Here's Life, 1981).

10. Larry D. Baker, "Delegating Effectively for Better Results," *The Management Team*, ed. Dorothy M. Walters (Glendora, CA: Royal Cassettes, Books, and Speakers, Inc., 1984), 211.

11. The idea for these examples came from Orville E. Easterly, "How Delegated Work Boomerangs," *Leadership Journal* (Spring 1989): 40–41, http://www.christianitytoday.com/le/1989/spring/89l2040.html.

Chapter 12 How to Break the 800 Barrier

1. I also explain these concepts in far greater detail in *Prepare Your Church for the Future*, chapter 9, 119–49, and all across *The Coming Church Revolution: Empowering Leaders for the Future* (Revell, 1994). In addition, see Charles Tidwell, *Church Administration*, 106–7.

2. A good starting point is two books by George Barna, *Marketing the Church: What They Never Taught You about Church Growth* (Colorado Springs: NavPress, 1988) and *Church Marketing: Breaking Ground for the Harvest* (Ventura, CA: Regal, 1992). Other solid tools are Norman Shawchuck, Philip Kotler, Bruce Wrenn, and Gustave Rath, *Marketing for Congregations: Choosing to Serve People More Effectively* (Nashville: Abingdon, 1992); Robert Bask, *Attracting New Members* (New York: Reformed Church of America, 1988); and a secular title, Carl Sewell, *Customers for Life* (New York: Doubleday, 1990).

3. George, *Prepare Your Church for the Future*, 42–54.

4. See the public list of large churches at www.hartfordinstitute.org and also the annual lists of "top 100" largest and fastest growing churches published by *Outreach* magazine at www.outreachmagazine.com.

5. Lyle E. Schaller, *The Seven-Day-a-Week Church* (Nashville: Abingdon, 1992), 28.

6. See Leadership Network's page of resources at www.leadnet.org/megachurch.

7. Schaller, *Seven-Day-a-Week Church*, 149.

8. Schaller, *Choices for Churches* (Nashville: Abingdon, 1990), 87.

9. John N. Vaughan, "Characteristics of Growing Churches," *Growing Churches* (Sunday School Board of the Southern Baptist Convention) vol. 1 no. 2 (January–March 1991): 16.

10. John N. Vaughan, "Megamyths," *Christianity Today* vol. 34 no. 4 (March 5, 1990): 24.

11. Lyle E. Schaller, *Forty-Four Ways to Increase Church Attendance* (Nashville: Abingdon, 1988), 89. See also pages 12, 39, 45. See also Schaller, *Growing Plans*, 116; Schaller, *The Senior Minister* (Nashville: Abingdon, 1988), 110–14; Schaller, *Seven-Day-a-Week Church*, 106; and Schaller, *Looking in the Mirror: Self-Appraisal in the Local Church* (Nashville: Abingdon, 1984), 150.

12. A bit of history might be of interest here: One of North America's first sustained megachurches (defined as attendance of 2,000 or more adults and children) was First Baptist Church of Fort Worth, Texas, which reported a *Sunday school attendance* of 5,200 in 1928. The next record holder was Akron Baptist Temple of Akron, Ohio, which reported an average of 5,762 for Sunday school. By 1979 the largest Sunday school was First Baptist Church of Hammond, Indiana, pastored by Jack Hyles, which reported 15,101 people in average attendance (John N. Vaughan, *The Large Church* [Grand Rapids: Baker, 1985], 12–13, 54–59).

In the early 1970s, worship attendance became larger than Sunday school attendance in many of the nation's largest churches. From the late 1970s onward, North America's largest church in *worship attendance* was again First Baptist Church of Hammond, Indiana (Elmer L. Towns, John N. Vaughan, and David J. Seifert, *The Complete Book of Church Growth* [Wheaton: Tyndale, 1981], 95). During 1992 the top North American attendance average for on-campus weekend services was held by either First Baptist Church of Hammond or Willow Creek Community Church. Then for several years Lakewood Church of Houston was the nation's largest-attendance church. Today multisite churches have approached or passed its size, with Life.Church becoming the largest in 2014. Many (but not all) of the largest churches participate in the "Top 100" listings by *Outreach* (www.outreachmagazine.com).

For other megachurch statistics, see www.leadnet.org/world.

Chapter 13 How to Break the Care Barrier

1. This 80 percent figure is a rounded figure commonly cited by church growth researchers. For example, separate quotations from Win Arn, Kirk Hadaway, and Robert Dale are cited in *Reviving the Plateaued Church* by R. D. Baker, Truman Brown Jr., and Robert D. Dale (Nashville: Convention Press, 1992), 7. Even strongly evangelistic denominations report that most of their churches are not experiencing growth. For example, Southern Baptists found that between 1985 and 1990, only 30.2 percent of their churches grew, whereas 51 percent were plateaued and 18.8 percent declined. A plateau is "based on a membership change of plus or minus 10 percent during a five-year period," and a decline is "based on membership losses of over 10 percent during a five-year period" (Linda S. Barr, ed., *Southern Baptist Handbook 1991* [Nashville: Sunday School Board of the Southern Baptist Convention, 1991], 18, 141).

2. George Barna, *What Americans Believe* (Ventura, CA: Regal, 1991), 234.

3. In *Filling the Holes in Our Souls* (Chicago: Moody, 1992) coauthors Paul Meier, Gene A. Getz, Richard A. Meier, and Allen R. Doran describe the "small group revolution" as "what may be the most significant phenomenon in the Christian church in the late twentieth century" (20).

4. A free online database of over five hundred global megachurches is maintained by Warren Bird through Leadership Network at www.leadnet.org/world. A significant earlier chronicler is John N. Vaughan, who documented the world's largest churches by size, describing them in a video series entitled *Megachurches of the World,* available at www.church growthtoday.com, and in his book *The World's Twenty Largest Churches* (Grand Rapids: Baker, 1984). I summarize them in my book *Prepare Your Church for the Future,* 50–51.

5. As cited in "To Verify . . . ," *Leadership Journal* vol. 12 no. 2 (Spring 1991): 114, and taken from *American Demographics* vol. 12 no. 11 (November 1990). Schaller poses the question, "Are there too many churches?" and gives a statistical rationale for answering in *The Small Church* Is *Different!*, 126–29.

6. Contact Stephen Ministries, www.stephenministries.org.

7. See George, *Prepare Your Church for the Future,* 31–33.

8. "Church Growth Fine Tunes Its Formulas," *Christianity Today* vol. 35 no. 7 (June 24, 1991): 47.

9. David Yonggi Cho, "Foreword" in John N. Vaughan's *The Large Church: A Twentieth-Century Expression of the First-Century Church* (Grand Rapids: Baker, 1985), 9.

10. Cho and Hostetler, *Successful Home Cell Groups,* 64.

11. "Church Growth," *Christianity Today,* 47.

12. "World Population Projected to Reach 9.7 Billion by 2050," United Nations Department of Economic and Social Affairs, July 29, 2015, http://www.un.org/en/development/desa/news/population/2015-report.html.

13. See the World Christian Database at http://www.worldchristiandatabase.org/wcd/. See also earlier statistics from Ralph D. Winter, U.S. Center for World Mission (Pasadena, CA), as summarized in such publications as *Mission Frontiers* (Jan.–Feb. 1992): 5.

Bibliography

Arn, Charles, and Gary McIntosh. *What Every Pastor Should Know: 101 Indispensable Rules of Thumb for Leading Your Church*. Grand Rapids: Baker, 2013. 272 pages.

> Includes excellent guidance on how many groups a church can support and how to identify potential group leaders.

Arn, Win, and Charles Arn. *The Master's Plan for Making Disciples*. Pasadena, CA: Church Growth Press, 1982. 176 pages.

> Develops the *oikos* evangelism principle of identifying people movements which travel along natural webs of relationship.

Barna, George. *The Power of Vision: How You Can Capture and Apply God's Vision for Your Ministry*. Ventura, CA: Regal, 1992. 192 pages.

> Highlights such topics as how vision is different from mission, why a mission statement is not the same thing as vision, and practical steps to take in discovering and implementing God's unique vision for your ministry.

Beaumont, Susan. *Inside the Large Congregation*. New York: Rowman & Littlefield, 2011. 264 pages.

> Addresses five systems at work in what she calls the professional church (400–800 in worship attendance), the strategic church (800–1,200), and the matrix church (1,200–2,000).

Bennis, Warren, and Burt Nanus. *Leaders: The Strategies for Taking Charge*. New York: Harper & Row, 1985. 244 pages.

> Pivotal for understanding the distinction between being a leader, such as the senior pastor as primary vision caster, and a manager, such as a staff pastor who answers the how-to questions.

Chaney, Charles, and Ron Lewis. *Design for Church Growth*. Nashville: Broadman, 1977. 216 pages.

A practical guide for pastors and other church leaders. This book explains how growth is not an accident; it's something to be planned and worked for. Tools, step-by-step guidance.

Cho, David Yonggi, with Harold Hostetler. *Successful Home Cell Groups*. Plainfield, NJ: Logos International, 1981. 176 pages.

The founding pastor of the largest church in the history of Christendom introduces his story with these words: "Church growth is only a by-product. The real secret is home cell groups." This fascinating narrative is not so much a how-to book as a glimpse into the soul of Dr. Cho and the cell-group ministry he developed.

Cole, Neil. *Organic Leadership: Leading Naturally Right Where You Are*. Grand Rapids: Shapevine/Baker, 2010. 320 pages.

Argues that the division between clergy and laity is usually a harmful one and shows many ways to empower lay leaders.

Dale, Robert D. *To Dream Again*. Nashville: Broadman, 1981. 160 pages.

This resource targets plateaued churches, helping them analyze their patterns and move back into a pattern of growth.

Donahue, Bill. *Leading Life-Changing Small Groups*. Grand Rapids: Zondervan, 2009. 192 pages.

Explores the detailed steps, drawn from experiences at Willow Creek Community Church, for how to build a church *of* small groups, not just *with* small groups.

Easum, Bill. *Church Growth Handbook*. Nashville: Abingdon, 1995. 178 pages.

Here are twenty tested church-growth strategies that have been implemented by church consultant William Easum with more than 4,000 church leaders across the United States and Canada. Also provides diagnostic tools, which now can be used with *The Complete Ministry Audit*, also by Easum.

Easum, Bill, and Bil Cornelius. *Go Big: Lead Your Church to Explosive Growth*. Nashville: Abingdon, 2006. 129 pages.

Two veteran pastors, one mainline and one nondenominational, challenge readers to have a big vision, showing what strong, effective pastoral leadership looks like.

Easum, Bill, and Bill Tenney-Brittain. *Effective Staffing for Vital Churches*. Grand Rapids: Baker, 2012. 126 pages.

Highlights four core processes vital to church health and growth: bringing people to Christ and the church, retaining them, discipling them, and sending them back out into the world. If you want to multiply the leaders in your church and develop a mission-minded staff that does the same, this is the place to start.

Fletcher, Michael. *Overcoming Barriers to Growth: Proven Strategies for Taking Your Church to the Next Level.* Minneapolis: Bethany, 2007. 144 pages.

Drawing from experience with his own church and from years of working with other churches worldwide, the author explains how internal changes—not external ones—are the key to clearing these hurdles.

Fowler, Harry H. *Breaking Barriers of New Church Growth.* Rocky Mount, NC: Creative Growth Dynamics, 1988. 127 pages.

Case studies of Southern Baptist churches which have gone through what the author perceives as the 35 barrier, the 75 barrier, and the 125 barrier. Offers principles relevant to each stage.

Gaede, Beth Ann. *Size Transitions in Churches.* New York: Rowman & Littlefield, 2001. 180 pages.

How to navigate through growth barriers, especially in long-established churches.

Galloway, Dale, with Warren Bird. *On-Purpose Leadership: Multiplying Your Ministry by Becoming a Leader of Leaders.* Kansas City: Beacon Hill, 2001.

Outlines the leadership and cell group principles used to build the more than 5,000 attendance at New Hope Community Church, Portland, Oregon.

George, Carl F. *Prepare Your Church for the Future.* Edited by Warren Bird. Tarrytown, NY: Revell, 1991. 240 pages.

Foundational for anyone investigating the metachurch paradigm. It paints a broad picture of what a cell-group-driven church looks like, including insights on how celebration and cell interrelate. As it urges and inspires pastors to place a higher priority on the formation of lay leaders, it offers a specific infrastructure and a leadership training model for doing so.

George, Carl F., and Robert E. Logan. *Leading and Managing Your Church.* Tarrytown, NY: Revell, 1987. 192 pages.

How do we build an effective ministry team? How do we translate vision into reachable goals? How do we obtain widespread goal ownership? This book contains workable answers from authors who effectively blend biblical principles, sound management insights, and ministry-based practical experiences.

George, Carl F., with Warren Bird, *The Coming Church Revolution: Empowering Leaders for the Future.* Grand Rapids: Revell, 1994. 349 pages.

Explains in detail how a metachurch develops leaders at every level.

239

George, Carl F., with Warren Bird. *Nine Keys to Effective Small Group Leadership: How Lay Leaders Can Establish Dynamic and Healthy Cells, Classes and Teams*, revised and updated edition. Taylors, SC: CDLM, 2007. 216 pages.

> The simple truths of Scripture illustrated in these nine keys will unlock and open doors that make the difference in health, growth, vitality, energy, and life in your small group. Your group can thrive as you learn and apply these simple keys.

Gladen, Steve. *Small Groups with Purpose: How to Create Healthy Communities*. Grand Rapids: Baker, 2013. 240 pages.

> The pastor of small groups at Saddleback Church describes how to create a healthy and strategic small group ministry.

Hartwig, Ryan, and Warren Bird. *Teams That Thrive: Five Disciplines of Collaborative Church Leadership*. Downers Grove, IL: InterVarsity Press, 2015. 272 pages.

> Emphasizes the value of doing church as a team and shows practical applications for a healthy church senior leadership team.

Haugk, Kenneth C. *Antagonists in the Church: How to Identify and Deal with Destructive Conflict*. Minneapolis: Augsburg, 1988. 189 pages.

> Although only a very few people are antagonists, these individuals have the potential to disrupt and even destroy a church's mission and ministry. The author, a clinical psychologist who founded the Stephen Series system of lay caring, offers fresh insight and practical tools for coping with antagonism when it arises.

Hunter, Kent R. *Foundations for Church Growth*. New Haven, MO: Leader, 1983. 204 pages.

> One of the best introductions to church-growth principles. This is written from a Lutheran point of view, but the ideas are practical for all.

Mancini, Will, and Warren Bird. *God Dreams: 12 Vision Templates for Finding and Focusing Your Church's Future*. Nashville: B&H, 2016. 261 pages.

> Answers the "why" of needing a clear vision and then provides step-by-step guidance for how to frame your church's future.

Mann, Alice. *The In-Between Church: Navigating Size Transitions in Congregations*. New York: Rowman & Littlefield, 1998. 118 pages.

> Congregations experiencing size change often do not recognize the need to change culture and form as part of the successful adaptation process. Mann details the adjustments in attitude and practice that are necessary to support successful size change.

Martin, Kevin. *The Myth of the 200 Barrier: How to Lead through Transitional Growth*. Nashville: Abingdon, 2005. 135 pages.

> Drawing on sociological and anthropological studies about the significance of numbers in human organizations, the author, an Episcopal pastor, proposes practical steps that church leaders will want to take.

McGavran, Donald A., and Win Arn. *How to Grow a Church*. Ventura, CA: Regal, 1973. 180 pages.

> Cast in a question-and-answer format, this top seller summarizes the views of two leaders in the church-growth movement.

McGavran, Donald A., and George G. Hunter III. *Church Growth: Strategies That Work*. Nashville: Abingdon, 1980. 120 pages.

> One of the best primers on the church-growth movement, this book also provides practical tips on motivating people for growth, training laity, helping small churches grow, and planting new churches.

McIntosh, Gary. *Growing God's Church: How People Come to Faith Today*. Grand Rapids: Baker, 2016. 192 pages.

> Shows pastors and church leaders how people are actually coming to faith today. It covers factors such as the priorities churches set for themselves, the reality of churchless Christians, and the influence of pastors.

———. *One Size Doesn't Fit All: Bringing Out the Best in Any Church Size*. Grand Rapids: Revell, 1999. 176 pages.

> Explores how the role of the pastor, board, and congregation change with each different church size.

———. *Taking Your Church to the Next Level: What Got You Here Won't Get You There*. Grand Rapids: Baker, 2009. 224 pages.

> Explains the impact of age and size on churches and outlines the improvements that must be made at each point for a church to remain fruitful and faithful to its mission.

Neighbour, Ralph W. *Where Do We Go From Here?* Houston: Touch Publications, 1990. 463 pages.

> A passionate, theologically rooted appeal to build churches on the cell-church model. The author, who comes from a strongly programmatic background, offers case studies of huge cell churches around the world. His examples provide the reader with many how-to ideas and equipping tools.

Nicholas, Ron, ed. *Small Group Leader's Handbook*. Downers Grove, IL: InterVarsity, 1982. 194 pages.

> This collection of articles focuses on the specialized training skillsets needed to conduct vibrant small groups.

Peace, Richard. *Small Group Evangelism*. Downers Grove, IL: InterVarsity, 1985. 190 pages.

This book presents basic principles and then outlines a nine- to thirteen-week training program.

Scazzero, Pete, with Warren Bird. *The Emotionally Healthy Church: A Strategy for Discipleship That Actually Changes Lives*. Grand Rapids: Zondervan, 2003. 224 pages.

Shows how a church's leadership cannot be spiritually mature until they're also becoming emotionally mature.

Schaller, Lyle E. *Activating the Passive Church: Diagnosis and Treatment*. Nashville: Abingdon, 1961. 159 pages.

This book diagnoses the causes of church passivity and formulates a method for combating the problem. It also shows how to overcome loss of direction in a church.

———. *The Change Agent*. Nashville: Abingdon, 1972. 207 pages.

The author maps out a number of strategies that address the difficulties, processes, and results of change. Helpful insights for the inevitable tough times when a church, especially a long-established one, faces the challenge of innovation.

———. *Forty-Four Steps Up Off the Plateau*. Nashville: Abingdon, 1992. 180 pages.

Schaller defines a plateau as a stagnant holding point in the size and energy of a church—a level at which energy is focused entirely on maintenance of existing structures. He outlines forty-four steps needed to break the bonds that tie down such a church.

———. *Growing Plans: Strategies to Increase Your Church's Membership*. Nashville: Abingdon, 1983. 176 pages.

Effectively using an informative case-history approach to outline church-growth strategies, Schaller proposes that visitation evangelism is the ideal method of obtaining new members. He then outlines four other strategies for increasing the size of a church.

———. *Looking in the Mirror: Self-Appraisal in the Local Church*. Nashville: Abingdon, 1984. 206 pages.

"Frequently," says this veteran church consultant, "it's difficult or impossible for congregational leaders to agree on the role God is calling the church to fill unless they can agree on contemporary reality." This book provides a conceptual framework necessary for a church to self-appraise its ministry.

———. *The Middle Sized Church*. Nashville: Abingdon, 1985. 160 pages.

This is a companion volume to his books on the smaller church and the larger church. Schaller examines the personality and unique opportunities facing the church of several hundred, with particular attention to the denominational and long-established church.

———. *The Multiple Staff and the Larger Church*. Nashville: Abingdon, 1980. 142 pages.

Large churches are different in expectations, performance, staffing, and use of lay volunteers. Schaller fully describes the differences that mark the larger church and offers much specific advice to this specialized group.

———. *The Seven-Day-a-Week Church*. Nashville: Abingdon, 1992. 192 pages.

With brilliant insight and engaging description, Schaller reveals the reasons behind the worldwide emergence of megachurches. He describes characteristics of both the church and the kind of person who pastors it.

———. *Small Congregation, Big Potential: Ministry in the Small Membership Church*. Nashville: Abingdon, 2004. 220 pages.

Helps smaller congregations see themselves as possessed of pools of talent and expanding possibilities.

Schaller, Lyle, and Warren Bird. *Wisdom from Lyle E. Schaller: The Elder Statesman of Church Leadership*, Nashville, TN: Abingdon, 2012. 200 pages.

Summarizes key ideas, using quotes and case studies, from major themes in Schaller's writing. Also includes a short biography of Schaller's life and influence.

Sullivan, Bill M. *Ten Steps to Breaking the 200 Barrier*. Kansas City, MO: Beacon Hill, 1988. 99 pages.

Going beyond a solid theoretical base, and drawing on years of practical experience, the author provides useful how-to-do-it advice applicable to any church currently at "survival size." In 2005, he also wrote *New Perspectives in Breaking the 200 Barrier*.

Surratt, Chris. *Small Groups for the Rest of Us: How to Design Your Small Group System to Reach the Fringes*. Nashville: Thomas Nelson, 2015. 176 pages.

A veteran pastor offers practical, proven strategies on how to move "ungrouped" church people into biblically based communities.

Surratt, Geoff, Greg Ligon, and Warren Bird. *The Multisite Church Revolution: Being One Church in Many Locations*. Grand Rapids: Zondervan, 2006. 224 pages.

The leading book on the why and how of becoming one church in two or more locations.

———. *A Multisite Church Roadtrip: Exploring the New Normal*. Grand Rapids: Zondervan, 2009. 248 pages.

Offers an insider's tour of several multisite churches and the specific issues each has worked through.

Thumma, Scott, and Dave Travis. *Beyond Megachurch Myths: What We Can Learn from America's Largest-Attendance Churches*. San Francisco: Jossey-Bass, 2007. 226 pages.

Profiles various stereotypes of large churches, drawing from a huge research project on very large churches.

Towns, Elmer L., Ed Stetzer, and Warren Bird. *Eleven Innovations in the Local Church: How Today's Leaders Can Learn, Discern, and Move into the Future.* Glendora, CA: Regal, 2007.

Highlights new structures and creative leadership approaches to growing churches.

Wagner, C. Peter. *Leading Your Church to Growth: A Guidebook for Clergy and Laity*. Ventura, CA: Regal, 1984. 224 pages.

Addressing both pastors and the congregation, Wagner stresses the fact that strong pastoral leadership and people partnership are essential for dynamic church growth. Dr. Wagner advocates strong pastoral leadership to equip the laity for ministry and shows how this can be developed into a positive growth factor.

———. *Your Church Can Be Healthy*. Nashville: Abingdon, 1979. 120 pages.

A description and analysis of the causes and symptoms of eight major growth-inhibiting diseases found in North American churches.

———. *Your Church Can Grow: Seven Vital Signs of a Healthy Church*, rev. ed. Ventura, CA: Regal, 1980. 170 pages.

Wagner's first book on American church growth has now become a basic document in the field. It offers practical insight on how a church can grow.

———. *Your Spiritual Gifts Can Help Your Church Grow*. Ventura, CA: Regal, 1979. 272 pages.

This book, one of the most popular on the subject, examines twenty-seven different gifts. The discussions are both objective and practical.

Zunkel, C. Wayne. *Growing the Small Church: A Guide for Church Leaders*. Elgin, IL: David C. Cook, 1982. 100 pages.

An extremely practical manual with great artwork helpful for use in teaching others.

Subject Index

Scripture Index

Exodus

18:13–23—195
31:1–11—58
35:30—36:1, 58

Judges

20:13–18—58

2 Samuel

7—34–35

1 Kings

18 and 19—49–51
19:14—101

Psalms

23—54–55

Proverbs

9:9—118
18:15—118

Jeremiah

23:28—35

Matthew

7:7–8—47
9:38—32
13:24–33—54

16:18—25
16:19—105
18:20—210
22:37–40—122
28:18–20—122
28:19–20—98, 147, 188

Luke

9:23—143
19:10—147
22:31–34—143

John

4:35–38—43
10:3—99
13:35—212
15:4–8—89
15:11—143
16:7—210
21:16—99

Acts

Book of—66
3:11—155
5:42—155
20:28—99

Romans

12:4–8—127
12:8—99
15:2—99

1 Corinthians

3:1–15—99
12:1–12—210
12:12–27—127
12:28—99
14:12—99, 210
14:26—210

2 Corinthians

5:17–21—141
10:8—99
13:10—99

Galatians

6:10—127

Ephesians

2:4–10—141
2:8–10—143
4:11–12—118
4:12–13, 29—99
5:25–32—127

Philippians

4:12–13—141

Colossians

1:18—127
2:7—99

Meet the Authors

About Carl George

Carl George, an experienced pastor and church-growth consultant, served as longtime director of the Charles E. Fuller Institute of Evangelism and Church Growth in Pasadena, California. While at the Institute, he directed the training of church consultants, pastors, and staff members from over one hundred denominations.

His wide exposure to the challenges of congregational growth led to the invention of the metachurch system for visualizing congregations. His books *Prepare Your Church for the Future* and *The Coming Church Revolution* both explore how learnings from the largest international churches could be implemented in North America. *Leading and Managing the Local Church* and *How to Break Growth Barriers* have helped pastors learn to analyze and overcome internal limitations to growth. With these tools, churches of all sizes have been led to break through the ceilings that constrained them.

The principles he has authored to guide small group ministry have been foundational in numerous influential churches. *Nine Keys to Effective Small Group Leadership* serves to focus attention on developing small group leaders and coaches and strengthening the caring connections among members.

Recognized by his peers as consistently insightful and well ahead of his time, he has served as president of the American Society for Church Growth and seen several of his books translated and published in Europe, Asia, and South America. He resides with his wife, Grace, near Greenville, South Carolina.

His website is www.metachurch.com.

About Warren Bird

Warren Bird, PhD, after pastoring for fourteen years, oversees the research division of Leadership Network, the nation's leading organization to help entrepreneurial church leaders move from ideas to implementation to increased influence and impact. He is the award-winning author, coauthor, or editor of twenty-eight books for church leaders, over two hundred magazine articles, and several dozen groundbreaking church trend reports, available at www.leadnet.org.

Widely quoted in national media, he is one of the nation's leading scholars and writers on megachurches, multisite churches, high-visibility pastoral succession, and large church compensation. He is also a longtime adjunct professor at Alliance Theological Seminary, Nyack, New York.

Warren and his wife, Michelle, live just outside New York City.

Learn More about Carl George's Work at

WWW.CONSULTINGFORGROWTH.ORG

Author Warren Bird is Research Director at Leadership Network.

Leadership Network®

Where do you go for the ideas, connections, and inspiration needed for lasting Kingdom impact?

Learn more about Leadership Network:
leadnet.org

@leadnet

/leadnet.org

@leadnet

/leadershipnetwork